The Best Tastes In Scotland | 2005
Clark's Guide

In bringing together my choice of the Best Tastes in Scotland, I've been able to call on many years of valuable experience in the industry. I wanted to produce this book in the sincere hope that it will help guide you to the very best eating places that we have to offer.

Scotland is a wonderful country in so many ways, not the least being its claim to some of the finest produce and most highly skilled chefs and cooks in the world. This combination of ingredients and talent can result in some of the most extraordinary dining experiences available anywhere.

I am particularly keen to receive feedback from you. I hope you'll tell me about your experiences of visiting the establishments in the Guide and also suggest additional features that you would find valuable to include in the next edition.

And that's why I would encourage you to visit the Guide website at **www.besttastesinscotland.com** and register your details so that I can keep you informed of future developments. Failing that, please use one of the forms at the back of the Guide and send or fax it to me.

On my way to producing this Guide I have been lucky to enjoy the support of many colleagues and friends who have encouraged and cajoled me along the way. They know who they are and my thanks go to every one of you. In particular, I thank my family who have surpassed expectations with the support they have given me.

And finally, I would like to dedicate this first Guide to the memory of Tom – my husband and partner of more than 23 years and father of Carly, Rosie and Ben. His loss will always be felt – however the strength he showed in the face of adversity is a lesson to all of us who knew him.

Enjoy eating your way round Scotland and remember to tell me what you think.

Amanda J Clark

Credits

Published by
Amanda Clark Associates
c/o Frame Creative, 1–3 South East
Circus Place, Edinburgh EH3 6TJ
Email: amanda@amandaclark.co.uk
Web: www.amandaclark.co.uk

Designed and Produced by
Frame Creative, Edinburgh
Editorial: Jim Middleton
Design: David Healy
Special thanks to David Frame and
Jim Middleton for their support
and vision.

Printed by
Scotprint, Haddington, East Lothian

Amanda Clark is grateful for the
support of Baxters of Speyside, the
National Trust for Scotland and the
many establishments in the Scottish
Tourism Industry

Photography: Orkney Tourist Board,
Scottish Borders Tourist Board,
Aberdeen and Grampian Tourist
Board, The Townhouse Company,
Three Chimneys, Renzo Mazollini

Contents

Using the Guide

Selection process

All of the establishments listed in Clark's Guide are known to me personally or come highly recommended. I have used the following selectors for my criteria:

The establishment must have been known to me in the past 10 years through my time with Taste of Scotland and still be under the same ownership/management
or
The establishment must have been recognised by a quality national body
or
The establishment must have been recommended to me by a respected and known source.

During the writing of this Guide, it was an enormous pleasure to re-live many great dining and sociable experiences! I am aware, however, that standards can vary from time to time, so if your expectations are not met in any way, do let me know.

Opening times, etc.

As many of the businesses listed in my Guide are small owner-operators there may be occasions when the establishments are not open for business. For that reason – and the fact that in many cases a visit may involve a lengthy journey – I suggest you take the time to check in advance that the establishment will be open for business on the day you are planning to visit. This should ensure you are not disappointed.

It is also helpful to let them know in advance of any special requirements you and your party may have. This can range from specific dietary requirements to accessibility issues. Again, a moment spent in advance on this can save disappointment later.

How to use this Guide

There is an alphabetical index at the back of the Guide if you know the establishment you are looking for. Alternatively, all establishments are listed under the name of their nearest town/village. The map on Page 8 gives a general guide but it's not intended for use as a roadmap. As many of the places listed are at the end of small wonderfully winding roads, I would always urge you to use a good roadmap as well.

The Entries

All the entries have been written by me and not by the establishments themselves. I wanted to have a Guide that is not simply filled with advertorial from the establishments. I have endeavoured to ensure that the information is accurate at time of printing. The only information which was supplied to me are the details of any Awards and plaudits that the establishments have earned.

THE BEST TASTES
in Scotland 2005

A SELECTION OF THE FINEST PLACES TO EAT AND STAY

THE BEST TASTES
in Scotland 2005

Blairs Restaurant
Ardoe House Hotel
South Deeside Road
Aberdeen AB12 5YP
Tel 01224 8606600
Fax 01224 861283
email ardoe@macdonald-hotels.co.uk
Web www.macdonald-hotels.co.uk

A classic Scots baronial mansion with tasteful modern extensions, Ardoe House is located on the outskirts of Aberdeen on the south-west side. It is ideally located for leisure and business use with an impressive restaurant and excellent facilities. 2 AA Rosettes

Atholl Hotel
54 Kings Gate
Aberdeen AB15 4YN
Tel 01224 323505
Fax 01224 321555
email info@atholl-aberdeen.co.uk
Web www.atholl-aberdeen.com

Atholl House Hotel is in the heart of the city's West End. An attractive building, this hotel offers an excellent base for the business or leisure visitor with good, skilled cooking in the restaurant using local produce.

Seasons Restaurant
Craighaar Hotel
Waterton Road, Bucksburn
Aberdeen AB11 6UJ
Tel 01224 712275
Fax 01224 716362

email info@craighaar.co.uk
Web www.craighaarhotel.com

Craighaar Hotel is a charming hotel on the outskirts of the city, only five minutes from the airport. The restaurant and the bar offer dining of a very high standard in comfortable and welcoming surroundings.

The Fjord Inn
Fisherford, Aberdeen
Aberdeenshire AB51 8YS
Tel 01464 841232
Fax 01464 841232
email n.w.mundie@btinternet.com
Web www.thefjordinn.co.uk

The Fjord Inn is a great example of good Highland hospitality where friendly proprietors offer a genuinely warm welcome and the exemplary cooking employs only fresh local produce.

The Marcliffe at Pitfodels
North Deeside Road
Aberdeen AB15 9YA
Tel 01224 861000
Fax 01224 868860
email enquiries@marcliffe.com
Web www.marcliffe.com

The Marcliffe Hotel remains one of the best places to stay in Aberdeen. On the outskirts of the city it offers superb accommodation including new junior suites, amenities (including a new fitness room – January 2005) and service. Dining in the conservatory offers much to savour as the chefs use good local produce to its best advantage.

ABERDEEN

Old Mill Inn
South Deeside Road
Mary Culter
Aberdeen
AB12 5FX
Tel 01224 733212
Fax 01224 732884
email info@oldmillinn.co.uk
Web www.oldmillinn.co.uk

The Old Mill Inn is a great place to stop and enjoy quality Scottish ingredients, well cooked, in traditional surroundings.

ABERDEEN

Simpson's Hotel
59 Queens Road
Aberdeen AB15 4YP
Tel 01224 327777
Fax 01224 327700
email address@simpsonshotel.co.uk

Simpson's Hotel is centrally located in Queens Road and is an excellent, stylish place to base yourself while in Aberdeen. The standard of accommodation and surroundings is very high, the service is excellent and the cooking quite superb – skilled and innovative.

ABERDEEN

Victoria Restaurant
140 Union Street
Aberdeen
AB10 1JD
Tel 01224 621381

The Victoria Restaurant is centrally located on Union Street and is just the place to enjoy a quality and individual experience whether for lunch or a welcome break. Customers can enjoy tasty home baking or a light lunch in comfortable surroundings.

ABERFELDY

Farleyer House Hotel
Aberfeldy
Perthshire
PH15 2JE
Tel 01887820332
email info@farleyer.com
Web www.farleyer.com

Farleyer House is located amid some of Perthshire's most beautiful countryside. It is a particularly delightful property which has a modern bistro offering good food and wines – and the accommodation is of the highest standard. 2 AA Rosettes

ABERLOUR

Archiestown Hotel & Bistro
Archiestown
By Aberlour
Moray
AB38 7QL
Tel 01340 810218
Fax 01340 810239
email rmc@archiestownhotel.co.uk
Web www.archiestownhotel.co.uk

Archiestown Hotel is a village inn in the square of this delightful Speyside village. Accommodation is comfortable and the food in the pub is of very good quality – not to be missed

ABOYNE

The Boat Inn
Charlestown Road
Aboyne
Aberdeenshire AB34 5EL
Tel 013398 86137
email boatinnltd@aol.com

The Boat Inn has been here since the Jacobite rebellion and offers family-friendly hospitality in interesting surroundings. There is something here for every taste, from bar meals to the full dining experience.

ACHARACLE

Feorag House
Glenborrodale
Acharacle
Argyll PH36 4JP
Tel 01972 500248
Fax 01972 500285
email admin@feorag.demon.co.uk
Web www.feorag.co.uk

Feorag House is a delight, run by committed and caring owners Hospitality is of the highest standard with wonderful views to match. The food is equally impressive from afternoon tea on arrival to superb dining – well worth seeking out.

ACHILTIBUIE

Summer Isles Hotel
Achiltibuie
Ross-shire IV26 2YG
Tel 01854 622282
Fax 01854 622251
email Info@summerisleshotel.co.uk
Web www.summerisleshotel.co.uk

Summer Isles Hotel is just one of these very special places. For more than 20 years, it has been expertly run by the same owners who offer a memorable experience with cooking to match, and that's before we mention the views!

ALEXANDRIA

Sheildaig Farm
Upper Stoneymollen Road
Alexandria G83 8QY
Tel 01389 752459
Fax 01389 753695
email sheildaig@talk21.com
Web www.scotland2000.com/sheildaig

Formerly a working farm, Sheildaig Farm now offers a unique experience in delightful surroundings. The owners run this establishment to the highest of standards and offer a special, indeed unique dining experience.

ALFORD

Kildrummy Castle Hotel
Kildrummy, Alford
Aberdeenshire AB33 8RA
Tel 01975 571288
Fax 01975 571345
email bookings@
kildrummycastlehotel.co.uk

The village of Crovie on the Banffshire coast of the Moray Firth

Web www.kildrummycastlehotel.co.uk

Kildrummy Castle has been under the same ownership for many years and still maintains its reputation for offering a memorable country house experience in delightful surroundings. A high standard experience all round can be expected here.

ANSTRUTHER

The Anstruther Fish Bar
42-44 Shore Street
Anstruther
Fife
KY10 3AQ
Tel 01333 310518
email ansterfishbar@btconnect.com
Web www.anstrutherfishbar.co.uk

The Anstruther Fish Bar remains one of the best places in Scotland to enjoy great fresh fish suppers – whether you decide to eat in or take your meal out to the harbour this is one experience not to be missed. And don't be put off by the queues – they move along quickly!

ANSTRUTHER

The Cellar at Anstruther
Anstruther
Tel 01333 310378
Fax 01333 312544

Peter Jukes has a justifiable reputation for offering some of the best dining to be found in the East Neuk. With its highly skilled chef, this restaurant is a special experience where guests can enjoy the very best of local produce, skillfully prepared and in warm and welcoming surroundings.

ANSTRUTHER

The Spindrift Guest House
Pittenweem Road
Anstruther
KY10 3DT
Tel 01333 310573
Fax 01333 310573
email info@thespindrift.co.uk
Web www.thespindrift.co.uk

The Spindrift is a most welcoming guest house in this delightful East Neuk village where guests can enjoy good Scottish cooking in comfortable surroundings.

APPIN

Lochside Cottage
Fasnacloich, Appin
Argyll PA38 4BJ
Tel 01631 730216
Fax 01631 730216
email broadbent@
lochsidecottage.fsnet.co.uk
Web www.lochsidecottage.fsnet.co.uk

Make the most of Lochside Cottage while it remains one of Argyll's best-kept secrets. Guests are assured of a very warm welcome from attentive hosts in comfortable surroundings. Cooking is superb using only best Scottish ingredients.

APPLECROSS

Applecross Inn
Shore Street
Applecross IV54 8LR
Tel 01520 744262
Fax 01520 744400
email applecrossinn@globalnet.co.uk
Web www.applecross.net

The Applecross Inn offers a wide choice of snacks and meals with a speciality being excellent locally-caught fish, cooked and presented by a chef who clearly knows his subject well.

ARBROATH

The Corn Kist Coffee Shop
Milton Haugh, Carmyllie
By Arbroath
Angus DD11 2QS
Tel 01241 860579
Fax 01241 431633
Web www.miltonhaugh.com

Corn Kist Coffee Shop is a family-run business which offers the best of home-made goods and all using local ingredients. One of these real 'finds' when you're looking for good quality at reasonable prices.

ARDLUI

The Stagger Inn
Inverarnan
Ardlui
by Arrochar G83 7ZZ
Tel 01301 704274

The Stagger Inn is a pub with a sense of character all of its own. It is ideally located to provide you with a hearty bar meal to fortify you while you're exploring this delightful part of Scotland.

ARISAIG

Old Library Lodge and Restaurant
Arisaig
Inverness-shire PH39 4NH
Tel 01687 450657
email reception@olibrary.co.uk

The Old Library Lodge and Restaurant, run by Angela and Alan Broadhurst, lies in a most attractive situation. The hosts are committed to offering guests a unique experience with skilled cooking using only the very best produce.

ARRAN, ISLE OF

Apple Lodge
Lochranza
Isle of Arran KA27 8HJ
Tel 01770 830229
Fax 01770 830229

Apple Lodge is a charming house set in its own gardens. The accommodation is very comfortable and the ambience is relaxed and informal. Cooking here is to a very fine standard indeed; great care is taken with local produce and much skill and enthusiasm is in evidence.

ARRAN, ISLE OF

Garden Restaurant
Auchrannie Country House Hotel
Brodick
Isle of Arran
KA27 8BZ
Tel 01770 302234
Fax 01770 302812
email ijohnston@auchrannie.co.uk
Web www.auchrannie.co.uk

Auchrannie Country House Hotel is a very comfortable hotel which also has superb lodges for those who prefer self catering. The amenities here are excellent, ensuring there is plenty to do whatever the weather. Informal and formal dining are available and both equally offer a high standard of cooking, skilful presentation and use of local produce.

ARRAN, ISLE OF

Brodick Castle Restaurant
Brodick
Isle of Arran
KA27 8HY
Tel 01770 302202
Fax 01770 302312
email kthorburn@nts.org.uk
Web www.nts.org.uk

Brodick Castle is another National Trust property which is a delightful destination with superb views. The restaurant is in the castle itself and offers an appealing range of home baking, snacks and light meals all using good local ingredients and served by friendly and welcoming staff.

The Traquair Arms at Innerleithen

ARRAN, ISLE OF

Kilmichael Country House Hotel
Glen Cloy
by Brodick
Isle of Arran KA27 8BY
Tel 01770 302219
Fax 01770 302068
email enquiries@kilmichael.com
Web www.kilmichael.com

Kilmichael Country House is a real gem, a beautifully-furnished country house in delightful gardens where comfort is a priority. The cooking here is highly skilled and the dishes are beautifully presented in the comfortable and elegant dining room.

ARRAN, ISLE OF

Sannox Bay Hotel
Sannox
Isle of Arran KA27 8JD
Tel 01770 810225
Fax 01770 810638
email sannoxbayhotel@connectfree.co.uk
Web www.sannoxbayhotel.co.uk

Sannox Bay Hotel sits in a prime position with sea views. The bar has a friendly atmosphere and is just the place to enjoy a good bar meal. Food is freshly prepared and locally sourced.

AUCHTERARDER

Andrew Fairlie @ Gleneagles
The Gleneagles Hotel
Auchterarder
Perthshire
PH3 1NF
Tel 01764 694267
Fax 01764 694163
email andrew.fairlie@gleneagles.com

This has to be one of the finest dining experiences to be enjoyed in Scotland. If you value the very best surroundings, superb skilled cooking and excellent service then you should make a booking at this icon of quality!

AUCHTERARDER

The Dormy Clubhouse – Gleneagles
The Gleneagles Hotel
Auchterarder
Perthshire
PH3 1NF
Tel 01764 662231
Fax 01764 662134
email alan.j.hill@gleneagles.com
Web www.gleneagles.com

The Dormy Clubhouse is an ideal place to enjoy the special atmosphere of Gleneagles whether between rounds of golf or perusing the delights of Perthshire. Something for everyone here whether à la carte or from the hot buffet.

AUCHTERARDER

Duchally Hotel
By Gleneagles
Auchterarder
Perthshire
PH3 1PN
Tel 01764 663071
email dcampbell@clublacosta.com

Duchally is a delightful hotel in this stunning part of Perthshire. Unobtrusive and welcoming, this is one place to enjoy comfortable surroundings and excellent cooking.

AUCHTERHOUSE, BY DUNDEE

East Mains House
The Music Room Restaurant
Auchterhouse, by Dundee
Angus DD3 0QN
Tel 01382 320206
Fax 01382 320206
email dfrangus@aol.com

A former factor house of the Airlie Estate, this establishment offers a superb experience in interesting surroundings. Only the best Scottish produce is used here, some even from the grounds, all skilfully prepared and presented.

Corrour House Hotel
Rothiemurchus
by Aviemore PH22 1QH
01479 810220
Fax 01479 811500
email enquiries@corrourhousehotel.co.uk
Web www.corrourhousehotel.co.uk

Corrour House is a delightful family-run country house hotel which offers good value, comfortable surroundings and great views. The owners provide their visitors with imaginative Scottish country cooking and the number of repeat guests is a testament to their success.

The Old Bridge Inn
23 Dalfaber Road
Aviemore PH22 1PU
Tel 01479 811137
Fax 01479 810270
email nreid@
highlandcateringresources.co.uk
Web www.oldbridgeinn.co.uk

The Old Bridge Inn is located just on the outskirts of Aviemore and offers simply cooked good Scottish fare across a range of bar meals. Well worth seeking out whilst in the area.

Ptarmigan Restaurant
Cairngorm Mountain
by Aviemore
Inverness-shire PH22 1RB
Tel 01479 861334
Fax 01479 861207

email heather@cairngormmountain.com
Web www.cairngormmountain.com

The Ptarmigan Restaurant has to be one of the most unusual places in Scotland to enjoy a good meal. Your appetite is whetted by the ride up the Cairngorm Mountain funicular railway and then you enjoy the stunning views complemented by good Scottish fare.

The Rowan Tree Country Hotel
Loch Alvie
By Aviemore PH22 1QB
Tel 01479 810207
Fax 01479 810207
email enquiries@rowantreehotel.com
Web www.rowantreehotel.com

The Rowan Tree Hotel offers good Highland hospitality. A concise menu offers local specialities freshly cooked and skilfully presented. A tearoom adjacent to the hotel also offers good home baking and snacks.

The Fruits de Mer
38 North Harbour Street
Ayr KA8 8AH
Tel 01292 282962
Fax 01292 290877
Web www.fruits-de-mer.co.uk

Although Fruits de Mer is, as you would expect, a fish restaurant, menus also include meat and vegetarian dishes. Run by a fisherman turned chef, you can be sure the produce is carefully handled.

Castle Fraser, Inverurie, Aberdeenshire

AYR

Café Ivy
The Ivy House Hotel
2 Alloway
Ayr KA7 4NL
Tel 01292 442336
Fax 01292 445572
email enquiries@theivyhouse.uk.com
Web www.theivyhouse.uk.com

The Ivy House is set back from the road overlooking the countryside and golf courses. Here you can enjoy anything from simple snacks to the very best dining experience overseen by a highly skilled chef in delightful surroundings.

AYR (OUTSKIRTS)

Enterkine House
Annbank
By Ayr KA6 5AL
Tel 01292 521608/520580
Fax 01292 521582
email mail@enterkine.com
Web www.enterkine.com

Enterkine House is a gracious building in delightful grounds. A great choice to enjoy professional, discreet service and superb cooking whether your stay is for golf, business or simply pleasure.

BALLACHULISH

Ballachulish House
Ballachulish
Argyll PH49 4JX
Tel 01855 811266
Fax 01855 811498
email mclaughlins@btconnect.com
Web www.ballachulishhouse.com

Ballachulish House is a real delight.

Sitting in the most stunning surroundings, this is a special place where guests can enjoy excellent food, using superb produce and the very highest standards of Highland hospitality.

BALLACHULISH

Glencoe Visitor Centre
Glencoe
Ballachulish
Argyll
PH49 4LA
Tel 01855 811307/811729
Fax 01855 812010
email sborland@nts.org.uk
Web www.nts.org.uk

This environmentally friendly visitor centre is a 'must-see' when passing through Glencoe. The self-service restaurant has a good selection of soups, light snacks and home baking.

BALLANTRAE

Cosses Country House
Cosses
Ballantrae
Ayrshire
KA26 0LR
Tel 01465 831363
Fax 01465 831598
email info@cossescountryhouse.com
Web www.cossescountryhouse.com

Cosses Country House is justifiably recognised as one of our best small country houses, offering the very highest standard of accommodation and hospitality. Susan is a highly accomplished cook and prepares only the best fresh produce with imagination and skill for her guests. Winner Les Routiers Best B&B in Scotland 2003. Macallan Award 2000.

Auld Kirk Hotel
Braemar Road
Ballater AB35 5RQ
Tel 013397 55762
Fax 013397 55707
email auldkirkhotel@aol.com
Web www.auldkirkhotel.com

The Auld Kirk Hotel is a former church, tastefully converted to provide a high standard of accommodation and dining facilities. It is popular with visitors and locals and the delicious meals incorporate local produce with flair.

Balgonie Country House Hotel
Braemar Place
Ballater AB35 5NQ
Tel 013397 55482
Fax 013397 55497
email balgoniech@aol.com
Web www.balgoniech@aol.com

Balgonie has been run by John and Priscilla Finnie for many years and has a well-earned reputation with its guests for offering the highest standards of hospitality in comfortable surroundings. The cooking is skilled and imaginative using best local produce. STB 4 Star Small Hotel, AA 2 Star, AA 2 Rosettes

Crannach Coffee Shop & Gallery
Cambus O'May, Ballater
Aberdeenshire AB35 5SD
Tel 01339 755126
email info@crannach-culture.co.uk

Crannach Coffee Shop and Gallery is a great place to stop whilst exploring the area. It is open all day and offers a good range of home baking, cooking, snacks and meals. The home baking is especially recommended.

Darroch Learg Hotel
Braemar Road
Ballater
Aberdeenshire AB35 5UX
Tel 013397 55443
Fax 013397 55252
email nigel@darrochlearg.co.uk
Web www.darrochlearg.co.uk

Darroch Learg, run by Nigel and Fiona Franks, has a long tradition of offering the very best of everything – from the comfortable surroundings to the excellent and highly skilled cooking.

Deeside Hotel
Braemar Road
Ballater AB35 5RQ
Tel 013397 55420
Fax 013397 55357
email deesidehotel@btconnect.com
Web www.deesidehotel.co.uk

The Deeside Hotel is a small, family-run hotel which offers good quality in the bar, restaurant and conservatory. It is comfortable and welcoming and well worth a visit.

BALLATER

Glen Lui Hotel
Invercauld Road, Ballater
Aberdeenshire
AB35 5RP
Tel 013397 55402
email infos@glen-lui-hotel.co.uk

The Glenlui is owned by Serge and Lorraine Geraud and the French influence here only enhances its charm. Service is friendly and welcoming and the menus are varied using good local produce with a continental twist.

BALLATER

Loch Kinord Hotel
Dinnet
Nr Ballater
Royal Deeside AB34 5JT
Tel 01339 885229
Fax 01339 887007
email info@kinord.com
Web www.lochkinord.com

Loch Kinord Hotel is situated just on the outskirts of Ballater and provides excellent dining in the restaurant. A full à la carte menu is offered in the modern Scottish style, using the best ingredients with skill.

BALLATER

Station Restaurant
Station Square
Ballater AB35 5QB

Tel 013397 55050

As its name would suggest this is a converted station dining room. Owned by the same family as Darroch Learg, the Station Restaurant is an ideal venue to enjoy home baking, good quality refreshments, snacks and meals.

BALLOCH

The Stables Restaurant
Roundabout Inn
Carrochan Road
Balloch
G83 8BW
Tel 01389 752148
Fax 01389 755032
email info@stablesrestaurant.com
Web www.stablesrestaurant.com

The Stables Restaurant at Balloch has maintained its reputation for more than 30 years and continues to satisfy its customers with a commitment to good value, good service and good food. Menus are comprehensive and offer something to suit all tastes and ages.

BALMEDIE

Cock & Bull
Ellon Road
Blairton
Balmedie
AB23 8XY
Tel 01358 743249
Fax 01358 742466

Cock & Bull offers high standards of service and hospitality in traditional surroundings. Cooking is accomplished with an international influence from snacks, lunches, afternoon teas and dinner.

BALQUHIDDER

Monachyle Mhor Hotel & Restaurant
Balquhidder, Lochearnhead
Perthshire FK19 8PQ
Tel 01877 384622
Fax 01877 384305
email info@monachylemhor.com
Web www.monachylemhor.com

The Lewis family have a well-deserved reputation for offering a superb level of hospitality and welcome to their guests. Tom is a highly accomplished chef and uses only the best local produce which he prepares with flair and imagination.

BANAVIE

An Crann B&B and Restaurant
Seangan Bridge, Banavie
Fort William PH33 7PB
Tel 01397 773114
email seangan-chalets@
fortwilliam59.freeserve.co.uk

An Crann is a B&B and Restaurant run by the Ross family. Here the best Highland hospitality is offered in the carefully converted surroundings of an old stone barn. Cooking is good Scottish with a combination of modern and traditional dishes

BANCHORY

Horsemill Restaurant
Crathes Castle
Banchory
Aberdeenshire AB31 3QJ
Tel 01330 844525
Fax 01330 844797
email amitchell@nts.org.uk

Web www.nts.org.uk

No visit to Crathes Castle is complete without calling in to the Horsemill Restaurant. A good range of home baking, snacks and meals are on offer all day all using good Scottish ingredients and served by friendly welcoming staff.

BANCHORY

Raemoir House Hotel
Raemoir
Banchory
AB31 4ED
Tel 01330 824884
Fax 01330 822171
email enquiries@raemoir.com
Web www.raemoir.com

Raemoir House Hotel is set in 3500 acres of parkland, a particularly appealing location. The house itself has been tastefully furnished and decorated, making it a comfortable and relaxing choice, all of which is complemented by excellent cooking by an accomplished Chef.

BANCHORY

St Tropez
22d Bridge Street
Banchory
AB31 5SX
Tel 01330 822216
email kmouti@amserve.net

St Tropez is, as it sounds, a French restaurant in this Deeside town. This is a particularly good establishment where the cooking is skilled and all using fresh ingredients.

BANFF

The Bay Restaurant
Banff Springs Hotel
Golden Knowes Road
Banff
AB45 2JE
Tel 01261 812881
Fax 01261 815546

email info@banffspringshotel.co.uk
Web www.banffspringshotel.co.uk

With superb views of the Buchan coastline, Banff Springs Restaurant is a particularly good place to enjoy the location and the skilled cooking from the kitchen. Menus offer traditional Scottish food deftly prepared.

BANKFOOT

The Spiral Restaurant
Main Street
Bankfoot
Perth
PH1 4AA
Tel 01738 787778
email spiralrestaurant@aol.com

The Spiral Restaurant is a small, popular, family-run establishment on the outskirts of Perth. There is a wide range of refreshments on offer here – from snacks to light lunches and full three-course meals all simply prepared and presented. Family friendly and newly-opened beer garden.

BANKNOCK

Glenskirlie House
Kilsyth
Banknock
FK4 1UF
Tel 01324 840201
Fax 01324 841054
email macaloneys@glenskirliehouse.com
Web www.glenskirliehouse.com

This elegant country house is justifiably popular with locals and visitors to the area. The main formal dining room offers a highly professional standard of service and superb cooking. There is also a bar for more informal meals where the standard is equally high.

BEAULY

Lovat Arms Hotel
Beauly
Inverness-shire
IV4 7BS
Tel 01463 782313
Fax 01463 782862
email info@lovatarms.com
Web www.lovatarms.com

Lovat Arms Hotel is owned by the Fraser family and has a long and interesting history. This is a traditional hotel with a warm Scottish welcome, offering good Scottish cooking using Scottish produce.

BEAULY

Made In Scotland
Station Road
Beauly
IV4 7EH
Tel 01463 782578
Fax 01463 782409
email is@enterprise.net
Web www.madeinscotland.uk.com

A must for shopaholics in the area, the Made in Scotland restaurant offers a simple selection of snacks and light meals for the hungry shopper or traveller.

BIGGAR

Chancellor's Restaurant
Shieldhill Castle
Quothquan
Biggar ML12 6NA
Tel 01899 220035
Fax 01899 221092
email enquiries@shieldhill.co.uk
Web www.shieldhillcastle.com

Shieldhill Castle is a delightful place
with some parts dating back as far as
the 12th Century. It has been recognised
for the very high standards achieved in
the kitchen – and deservedly so – a
must-visit. 2 AA Rosettes

BIGGAR

Skirling House
Skirling, Biggar
Lanarkshire ML12 6HD
Tel 01899 860274
Fax 01899 860255
email enquiry@skirlinghouse.com
Web www.skirlinghouse.com

Skirling House is a delightful home
where guests are made to feel
particularly welcome. The surroundings
are very comfortable and are more
than matched by the very high
standards of cooking presented with
deft skill and care from the chef.

BIRNAM

Birnam Wood House
Perth Road, Birnam
By Dunkeld PH8 0BH
Tel 01350 727782
Fax 01350 727196
email bob@birnamwoodhouse.co.uk
Web www.birnamhouse.co.uk

Birnam Wood House is a very
comfortable guest house where you can
look forward to enjoying excellent
meals prepared and presented by an
accomplished cook. Ideal for those who
like good food, simply yet imaginatively
prepared in welcoming surroundings.

BIRNAM

Katie's Tearoom
Perth Road, Birnam
By Dunkeld PH8 0AA
Tel 01350 727223
Fax 01350 727154
email birnamauto@btinternet.com
Web www.birnamautopoint.co.uk

Katie's Tearoom is a good place to stop
for a refreshing break. Good home
baking, meals and snacks here, including
a take-away option on request.

BLACKFORD

Baxters at Tullibardine
Tullibardine, Blackford
Perthshire PH4 1QG
Tel 01343 820666
(for information pre-opening)
Web www.baxters.com
Hamper Freephone: 0800 1868 00

Opening Spring 2005, this new Baxters
experience will offer the most
extensive range of quality food and
gifts all under the one roof. Here you
will be able to enjoy a superb shopping
experience which will include a
Cashmere and Clothing hall, Cookshop,
Food Market and Gifts and Luxuries.

BLAIR ATHOLL

Rod & Reel Restaurant
The House of Bruar
Bruar Falls
Blair Atholl
Perthshire PH18 5TW
Tel 01796 483236
Fax 01796 483218
email office@houseofbruar.demon.co.uk

Web www.houseofbruar.com

What we did before the House of Bruar opened is hard to imagine. Ideally located just off the A9 this offers a good place to stop off – whether to break a journey or simply to enjoy the many varied delights available here. A very good range of snacks and meals are available on a self-service basis in comfortable surroundings.

BLAIR ATHOLL

The Loft Restaurant
Golf Course Road
Blair Atholl
by Pitlochry
PH18 5TE
Tel 01796 481377
Fax 01796 481511
Web www.theloftrestaurant.co.uk

The Loft Restaurant and Bistro offers skilfully prepared food in a choice of surroundings. Either one ensures a very high standard of dining experience whether informal in the Bistro or more formal in the Restaurant. One of these places which is well worth seeking out

BLAIRGOWRIE

Cargills Restaurant & Bistro
Lower Mill Street
Blairgowrie
Perthshire
PH10 6AQ
Tel 01250 876735
Fax 01250 876735
email exceed@btconnect.com
Web www.exceed.co.uk

Run by Willie Little (a highly

accomplished chef), this very good informal Bistro offers a wide range of dishes prepared with skill. Scottish is the theme here but with a modern twist.

BLAIRGOWRIE

Dalmunzie House Hotel
Spittal of Glenshee
Blairgowrie
Perthshire
PH10 7QG
Tel 01250 885224
Fax 01250 885225
email dalmunzie@aol.com
Web www.welcome.to/dalmunzie

Dalmunzie has been under the careful ownership of Simon Winton and his family for a good number of years. The hotel is set in many acres of grounds and offers a very wide range of facilities. Hospitality is warm and welcoming and the food is of very high quality, skilfully prepared and presented.

BLAIRGOWRIE

Drumnacree House Hotel & The Oven Bistro
St Ninians Road
Alyth
Blairgowrie
Perthshire
PH11 8AP
Tel 01828 632194
Fax 01828 632194
email derek@drumnacreehouse.co.uk
Web www.drumnacreehouse.co.uk

Drumnacree House is run to a very high standard and offers a unique experience. Much of the food served here is from the owners' own garden ensuring freshness and flavour. Cooking is skilled and menus are imaginative and interesting and food is well presented.

BLAIRGOWRIE

Kinloch House
By Blairgowrie
Perthshire
PH10 6SG
Tel 01250 884237
Fax 01250 884333
email reception@kinlochhouse.com
Web www.kinlochhouse.com

Kinloch House is a particularly beautiful country house which is elegantly and tastefully furnished and maintained. Now run by the Allen family it continues to be one of the best country houses in Scotland. Formerly from Airds at Appin – Graeme Allen is a highly skilled Chef and offers a very high standard of dining experience, using excellent produce.

BOAT OF GARTEN

The Boat
Boat of Garten
Inverness-shire
PH24 3BH
Tel 01479 831258
Fax 01479 831414
email holidays@boathotel.co.uk
Web www.boathotel.co.uk

The Boat Hotel is a great place to base yourself whilst in the area. The hotel is run by caring, hospitable hosts, the hotel itself is comfortable and tastefully upgraded with seven newly developed master rooms. The food offered in the Restaurant is highly skilled and stylishly presented. Commended as 'Rising Star' for 2004 by Scottish Hotel Review

BONNYRIGG, NR EDINBURGH

The Orangery
Dalhousie Castle & Spa
Bonnyrigg, nr Edinburgh
Midlothian EH19 3JB
Tel 01875 820153
Fax 01875 821936
email enquiries@dalhousiecastle.co.uk
Web www.dalhousiecastle.co.uk

Dalhousie Castle is a seriously romantic venue, which dates back to the 13th Century. There are two dining options here – more informal in the Orangery and more formal in the Dungeon Restaurant. Both offer very good food, skilfully prepared and presented.

BOTHWELL

Grapevine Restaurant & Wine Bar
27 Main Street
Bothwell G71 8RD
Tel 01698 852014
Fax 01698 854405

The Grapevine Restaurant has been serving locals and visitors for years – a testament to quality in itself. Food here is good but unpretentious and served in informal surroundings.

BRAEMAR

Gordon's Tearoom and Restaurant
20 Mar Road, Braemar
Aberdeenshire AB35 5YL
Tel 013397 41247
Fax 013397 41247
email iainboyd@totalise.co.uk

Gordon's Tearoom and restaurant offers traditional homely fare in comfortable surroundings. A range of snacks, light meals and more substantial dishes are offered here, all simply prepared. Home baking a speciality.

BRIDGE OF ALLAN

Epicures
Royal Hotel
55 Henderson Street
Bridge of Allan FK9 4HG
Tel 01786 832284
Fax 01786 834377
email stay@royal-stirling.co.uk
Web www.royal-stirling.co.uk

The Royal Hotel has something for everyone. Whether you are looking for a bar meal or something more formal you will not be disappointed. This is a very good hotel, operating to a high standard.

BRIDGE OF ORCHY

Bridge of Orchy Hotel
Bridge of Orchy
Argyll PA36 4AD
Tel 01838 400208
Fax 01838 400313
email info@bridgeoforchy.co.uk
Web www.scottish-selection.co.uk

Bridge of Orchy Hotel is very popular with walkers and tourists. This hotel has been tastefully refurbished and offers good wholesome Scottish food for the hungry visitor. The bar is also a good place to enjoy a wee malt!

BRIDGE OF WEIR

The Lochnagar
Main Street, Bridge of Weir
Renfrewshire PA11 3LA
Tel 01505 613410
Fax 01505 613410
email jwhrankin@lycos.co.uk

The Lochnagar does something very well that we Scots really enjoy. It offers good home baking and cooking in a friendly relaxed atmosphere. This is a particularly welcome place for those with children

who are well catered for – allowing parents to enjoy the experience.

BRORA

Royal Marine Hotel
Golf Road, Brora
Sutherland KW9 6QS
Tel 01408 621252
Fax 01408 621181
email info@highlandescape.com
Web www.highlandescapehotels.com

The Royal Marine Hotel is a distinctive property and is understandably popular with discerning golfers and other visitors. The food is very good Scottish with a modern twist in the café, bistro or more formal dining room.

BUCKIE

The Old Monastery Restaurant
Drybridge, Buckie
Moray AB56 5JB
Tel 01542 832660
Fax 01542 839437
email calum or val@oldmonastery.com
Web www.oldmonastery.com

The Old Monastery continues to thrive under the ownership of Calum and Val Buchanan. This fine restaurant (a converted church) serves the highest standard of Scottish food, all of which has been very carefully sourced, prepared and presented in comfortable surroundings.

BUTE, ISLE OF

The Bistro
Isle of Bute Discovery Centre
The Winter Garden
Victoria Street, Rothesay
Isle of Bute PA20 0AH
Tel 01700 505500

The Bistro is in a lovely setting and is an ideal place to enjoy fine cooking and great views across Rothesay Bay. Great care is taken in selecting only the best produce whether for light lunch or a more substantial lunch or dinner.

CAIRNDOW

Loch Fyne Oyster Bar
Clachan, Cairndow
Argyll PA26 8BL
Tel 01499 600236
Fax 01499 600234
email info@loch-fyne.com
Web www.lochfyne.com

Loch Fyne Oyster Bar is worth stopping at – even just to walk around. However it would be a shame not to really have the full experience and taste some of the superb seafood served in the restaurant. Equally of interest is the shop where you can take your selection home to enjoy.

CAITHNESS

Forss Country House Hotel
by Thurso
Caithness KW14 7XY
Tel 01847 861201
Fax 01847 861301
email jamie@forsshouse.freeserve.co.uk
Web www.forsscountryhouse.co.uk

Forss Country House is a family run country house hotel (home to the MacGregor family) which is popular with a range of visitors. The hotel is relaxing and comfortable and the cooking is traditional Scottish using good local ingredients.

CALLANDER

Creagan House Restaurant with Accommodation
Strathyre, Callander
Perthshire FK18 8ND
Tel 01877 384638
Fax 01877 384319
email eatandstay@creaganhouse.co.uk
Web www.creaganhouse.co.uk

Creagan House has been lovingly run by Gordon and Cherry Gunn for many years and has been appropriately recognised as such. This is a unique establishment on the outskirts of Strathyre, which has a quite stunning Baronial dining room. Gordon is an accomplished and highly skilled Chef and Cherry is a most welcoming host. 2 AA Rosettes, Red Star

CALLANDER

Dochfour
Strathyre
Callander FK18 8NA
Tel 01877 384256
Fax 01877 384256
email tony.ffinch@tesco.net

Dochfour is a well-run guest house which is run by very committed owners. The house is comfortable and relaxing and everything from the extensive breakfast menu to dinner is home made – good food not to be missed. Packed lunches also available.

CALLANDER

Poppies Restaurant
Leny Road, Callander
Perthshire FK17 8AL
Tel 01877 330329
Fax 01877 330329
email poppieshotel@yahoo.co.uk
Web www.scotland2000.com/poppies

Poppies Restaurant is located at the west end of the main road through Callander. It is a stylish restaurant which serves modern Scottish dishes – using local ingredients, well prepared and presented.

CALLANDER

Roman Camp Country House Hotel
Callander FK17 8BG
Tel 01877 330003
Fax 01877 331533
email mail@roman-camp-hotel.co.uk
Web www.roman-camp-hotel.co.uk

Roman Camp hotel is an exceptionally fine country house which has been run by the Brown family for many years. The surroundings are opulent and formal with service and dining to match. The cooking here is, as you might expect, highly skilled and well worth sampling.

CALLANDER

Rosebank House
Strathyre, by Callander
Perthshire FK18 8NA
email rosebankhouse@onetel.com

Rosebank House is a very comfortable guest house with magnificent views. The owners have ensured that guests' every comfort is allowed for and as such offer a unique and very pleasurable experience. Everything here is homemade from the home bakes to preserves. Produce is carefully sourced and skilfully cooked.

CARNOUSTIE

11 Park Avenue
11 Park Avenue, Carnoustie
Angus DD7 7JA
Tel 01241 853336
email parkavenue@oz.co.uk
Web www.11parkavenue.co.uk

Stephen Collinson has been deservedly recognised for his skill in the kitchen. This is a very special restaurant where the warm welcoming interior is complemented by a stunning eating experience. This is one of Scotland's little gems and not to be missed. 1AA Rosette, Michelin Red Guide.

CARNOUSTIE

The Dalhousie Restaurant
Carnoustie Hotel, Golf Resort & Spa
The Links

Carnoustie
Angus DD7 7JE
Tel 01241 411999
Fax 01241 411998
email enquiries@carnoustie-hotel.com
Web www.carnoustie-hotel.com

Carnoustie Hotel is a must for the golf enthusiast. This modern, very comfortable hotel is run to a very high standard to ensure it meets the demands of discerning guests. Menus are sophisticated and skilfully prepared and presented by a talented team.

CARRADALE

Dunvalanree
Port Righ Bay
Carradale
Kintyre
Argyll PA28 6SE
Tel 01583 431226
Fax 01583 431339
email eat@dunvalanree.com
Web www.dunvalanree.com

Dunvalanree is a popular family-run establishment. The hotel itself is set on a cliff affording excellent views of the bay and is comfortable and thoughtfully furnished. All food here is locally sourced and the cooking is very good indeed.

CARRADALE

Network Tea Room and Heritage Centre
Carradale
Heston
Argyll
PA28 6SG
Tel 01583 431296 or 01583 431278
Fax 01583 431419
email stuartirvine@talk21.com

The Network Tearoom is ideally located beside the Heritage Centre where local sealife and wildlife is celebrated. It is popular with locals and visitors and offers a range of home made soups, lights snacks and good home baking.

CARRBRIDGE

Conservatory Restaurant at Fairwinds
The Fairwinds Hotel
Carrbridge
Inverness-shire PH23 3AA
Tel 01479 841240
Fax 01479 841240
email enquiries@fairwindshotel.com
Web www.fairwindshotel.com

Fairwinds Hotel is a converted manse
run by hospitable owners. The dining
room is in a spacious conservatory and
the cooking is simply prepared Scottish
produce enhanced with a light touch. A
very good standard and most enjoyable
place to stay. Hotel Review Scotland.
Silver Award for Food. Breakfast
Rosettes. Red H Award for hospitality

CASTLE DOUGLAS

Craigadam
Castle Douglas DG7 3HU
Tel 01556 650233
Fax 01556 650233
email inquiry@craigadam.com
Web www.craigadam.com

Celia Pickup runs Craigadam with flair and
elegance. The house is large and
comfortable and the hospitality here is
second to none. In addition to all of this
the home cooking and baking is balanced
and deftly prepared and presented.

CASTLE DOUGLAS

Balcary Bay Hotel
Auchencairn
nr Castle Douglas
Dumfries & Galloway DG7 1QZ
Tel 01556 640217

Fax 01556 640272
email reservations@
balcary-bay-hotel.co.uk
Web www.balcary-bay-hotel.co.uk

Balcary Bay Hotel is in the most
superb location – exceedingly close to
the water and thus the views
overlooking the bay are second to
none. The hotel is run by the Lamb
family who are experienced and
caring hosts. Dining in the restaurant
is a special occasion with good
Scottish produce skilfully and
imaginatively produced. 2 AA
Rosettes

CASTLE DOUGLAS

The Crown Hotel
25 King Street
Castle Douglas
DG7 1AA
Tel 01556 504831
Fax 01556 502031
email reception@thecrownhotel.co.uk
Web www.thecrownhotel.co.uk

The Crown Hotel is a good place to
enjoy an informal bar meal whilst
visiting this particularly appealing
part of Dumfries and Galloway. Daily
specials are interesting and reflect
the really good local produce
available.

CASTLE DOUGLAS

The Imperial Hotel
35 King Street
Castle Douglas
DG7 1AA
Tel 01556 502086
Fax 01556 503009
email david@thegolfhotel.co.uk
Web www.thegolfhotel.co.uk

Built as a Coaching Inn the Imperial
Hotel offers a good place to enjoy an
informal bar meal. Daily specials are
worth looking out for but all bar food
uses local produce and is served in an
informal relaxed manner.

CASTLE DOUGLAS

Longacre Manor
Ernespie Road
Castle Douglas DG7 1LE
Tel 01556 503576
Fax 01556 503886
email ball.longacre@btinternet.com
Web www.aboutscotland.co.uk/south/
longacre.html

This delightful Edwardian home is an excellent example of good Scottish hospitality. The surroundings are comfortable, the hosts are very welcoming and the food served here is very good – Scottish cooking simply prepared and presented.

CASTLE DOUGLAS

The Plumed Horse
Crossmichael
Castle Douglas
Tel 01556 670333

The Plumed Horse is another of the finest dining experiences to be enjoyed in Scotland and found in a most unusual setting. The cooking here is highly accomplished, only the very best local ingredients are used and all presented with style and aplomb. Worth a special visit.

CHIRNSIDE

Chirnside Hall Country House Hotel
Chirnside nr Duns
Berwickshire TD11 3LD
Tel 01890 818219
Fax 01890 818231
email chirnsidehall@globalnet.co.uk
Web www.chirnsidehallhotel.com

This splendid country house has been refurbished to the highest standard and offers warm hospitality in a relaxed style. The menus here do not disappoint offering the very best produce, particularly very local game, and all prepared and presented to the highest standard.

COLL, ISLE OF

Isle of Coll Hotel
Arinagour
Isle of Coll
Argyll PA78 6SZ
Tel 01879 230334
Fax 01879 230317
email collhotel@aol.com
Web www.collhotel.com

The Isle of Coll Hotel is one of those great places where the produce is landed at the bottom of the garden and takes no time before being offered on your plate. A very special place to enjoy!

COLONSAY, ISLE OF

The Isle of Colonsay Hotel
Isle of Colonsay
Argyll
PA61 7YP
Tel 01951 200316
Fax 01951 200353
email colonsay.hotel@pipemedia.co.uk
Web www.colonsay.org.uk

The Isle of Colonsay Hotel is one of the most isolated small hotels in the country and a listed building which has been tastefully upgraded. A good range of meals and snacks are available.

COMRIE

Deil's Cauldron
27 Dundas Street, Comrie
Perthshire
PH6 2LN
Tel 01764 670352
email brian@deilscauldron.co.uk
Web www.deilscauldron.co.uk

The Deil's Cauldron has a small bar, bistro and restaurant – all of which offer Scottish dishes with some continental influences. The standard here is good, the welcome sincere and friendly – standards set by the enthusiastic owners. On a fine day try out the newly constructed petanque court!

COMRIE

The Royal Hotel
Melville Square
Comrie PH6 2DN
Tel 01764 679200
Fax 01764 679219
email reception@royalhotel.co.uk
Web www.royalhotel.co.uk

The Royal is a very comfortable hotel, well run by an enthusiastic, highly professional team. Guests have several options for dining – however all offer a good standard of local produce prepared with style and some contemporary slants.

CONTIN, BY STRATHPEFFER

Coul House Hotel
MacKenzie's Restaurant
Contin, By Strathpeffer
Ross-shire IV14 9ES
Tel 01997 421487
Fax 01997 421845
email coulhouse@bestwestern.co.uk
Web www.milford.co.uk/
go/coulhouse.html

Coul House is a comfortable pavilion style mansion located in extensive grounds. It is a relaxing and welcoming place to stay. Meals here are traditional Scottish and the welcome is warm.

CRAIGELLACHIE

Craigellachie Hotel
Ben Aigan Restaurant
Craigellachie
Banffshire AB38 9SR
Tel 01340 881204
Fax 01340 881253
email info@craigellachie.com
Web www.craigellachie.com

Craigellachie Hotel – with its stunning location overlooking the Spey in the midst of whisky country – is very comfortable, run to a high standard, and guests are made to feel most welcome. The cooking is excellent and best use is made of local produce presented with skill and flair.

CRAOBH HAVEN

Lunga Estate
Craobh Haven
Argyll
PA31 8QR
Tel 01852 500237
Fax 01852 500639
email colin@lunga.demon.co.uk
Web www.lunga.com

Lunga Estate is an unusual estate mansion which is still family run and offers a wide range of accommodation from self-catering estate cottages or flats and rooms. Good home cooking using estate and local produce.

CRATHES

The Milton
Crathes, Banchory
Kincardineshire AB31 5QH
Tel 01330 844566
Fax 01330 844666
email reservations@themilton.co.uk
Web www.themilton.co.uk

The Milton restaurant, opposite the entrance to Crathes Castle, is well worth visiting. Menus are varied offering a balanced choice, staff are friendly and professional and overall the experience here is a good one.

CRIANLARICH

Ewich House
Strathfillan
Crianlarich
Perthshire FK20 8RU
Tel 01838 300300
Fax 01838 300300
email lizzi@ewich.co.uk
Web www.ewich.co.uk

Ewich House is a very comfortable and tastefully furnished guest house set in the Strathfillan Glen. Hosts are accomplished and welcoming and the cooking is good Scottish using fresh local ingredients.

CRIANLARICH

The Green Welly Stop
Tyndrum, Crianlarich
Perthshire FK20 8RY
Tel 01838 400271
Fax 01838 400330
email thegreenwellystop@
tyndrum12.freeserve.co.uk
Web www.thegreenwellystop.co.uk

The Green Welly Stop is an institution with those who travel this route to Oban and Fort William regularly. Family-run, this is a great place to break your journey and enjoy some good home cooking or home bakes. There is something for everyone, from light snacks to more substantial meals. A popular favourite.

CRIEFF

The Bank Restaurant
32 High Street, Crieff
Perthshire PH7 3BS
Tel 01764 656575
Fax 01764 656575
email billmcguigan@aol.com
Web www.thebankrestaurant.net

The Bank Restaurant is a small, very appealing restaurant run by a husband and wife team. As you would expect from the name, it is a tastefully converted bank building where Lilias offers a warm, welcoming service. Bill is a skilled chef who prepares wholesome local produce in a modern Scottish style. AA Rosette

CRIEFF

Crieff Hydro
Crieff
Perthshire PH7 3LQ
Tel 01764 651602
Fax 01764 653087
email stephenleckie@crieffhydro.com

Crieff Hydro is a vast hotel, family-run, with facilities to suit everyone. Justifiably popular with families through generations, it is one of the few places where several age groups can get together and all enjoy the experience. Food here is good – less formal in the Brasserie and more so in the main restaurant.

CRIEFF

McNees
23 High Street
Crieff PH7 3HU
Tel 01764 654582
Fax 01764 654582
email mc.nees@virgin.net

McNees deli and takeaway sandwich shop comes well recommended. This is an ideal place to stock up on good local produce including locally smoked fish and meat and wonderful Mellis cheeses!

CUMBERNAULD

The Castlecary House Hotel
Castlecary Road
Cumbernauld G68 0HD
Tel 01324 840233
Fax 01324 840233
email inquiries@castlecaryhotel.com
Web www.castlecaryhotel.com

Castlecary Hotel has been tastefully renovated to offer a high standard of surroundings to its guests. Menus here are simple and offer good traditional cooking and hearty portions. Castlecary is particularly popular with locals.

CUPAR

Ostlers Close Restaurant
Bonnygate
Cupar KY15 4BU
Tel 01334 655574
Web www.ostlersclose.co.uk

Ostlers Close is another of these Neuk gems which has been superbly run by Jimmy and Amanda Graham for many years. Jimmy is a passionate chef who takes pride in sourcing the highest quality local ingredients and Amanda is a warm and attentive host.

DALRY

Braidwoods
Drumastle Mill Cottage
By Dalry KA24 4LN
Tel 01294 833544
Fax 01294 833553
email keithbraidwood@bt.connect.com
Web www.braidwoods.co.uk

Keith and Nicola Braidwood have been rightly recognised for the qualities they have brought to the Scottish culinary scene. This is another of the very best places to eat in Scotland located in a very pleasant Ayrshire countryside setting. They make a great team who constantly strive to achieve the highest of standards.

DIRLETON

The Open Arms Hotel
Dirleton, East Lothian EH39 5EG
Tel 01620 850241
Fax 01620 850570
email openarms@clara.co.uk
Web www.openarmshotel.com

A family-owned country hotel, The Open Arms is in a delightful location in this pretty East Lothian village. The atmosphere is informal and the meals served here are imaginative and skilful.

DORNOCH

Auchlea Guest House
Dornoch
Sutherland IV25 3HY
Tel 01862 811524
email fionagarvie@yahoo.com
Web www.milford.co.uk/go/auchlea.html

Auchlea is a comfortable, welcoming

guest house with open views about a mile from the centre of Dornoch. Good home cooking is offered here, all freshly prepared and very satisfying.

DORNOCH

Mallin House Hotel
Church Street
Dornoch IV25 3LP
Tel 01862 810335
Fax 01862 810810
email mallin.house.hotel@zetnet.co.uk
Web www.users.zetnet.co.uk/
mallin-house

Mallin House Hotel is a great place for those who appreciate good hearty portions after a day's activities. Menus are comprehensive and offer something for all tastes, all of which is prepared with a commitment to quality in pleasant surroundings.

DORNOCH

The Royal Golf Hotel
The 1st Tee, Dornoch
Sutherland IV25 3LG
Tel 01862 810283
Fax 01862 810923
email rooms@morton-hotels.com
Web www.morton-hotels.com

Ideal for the golfer, The Royal Golf overlooks the first tee of the Royal Dornoch Golf Club. Menus are a combination of traditional and modern and are served with style.

DORNOCH

Skibo Castle Hotel
Dornoch, Sutherland
Tel 01862 894600

High on the list of the very best places in Scotland, Skibo is quite unique. No question whatsoever about the quality of experience offered here in all aspects. It represents a memorable experience!

DOUNE

Doune
Knoydart, By Mallaig
Inverness-shire PH41 4PL
Tel 01687 462667
Fax 01687 462667
email martin@doune-marine.co.uk
Web www.doune-knoydart.co.uk

Doune is an exceptional place where guests are assured of a truly individual and high quality experience. The location is superb, the surroundings very comfortable and the cooking and hospitality are superlative.

DRYMEN

**Buchanan Arms Hotel &
Leisure Club**
Main Street, Drymen
Stirlingshire G63 0BQ
Tel 01360 660588
Fax 01360 660943
email enquiries@buchananarms.co.uk
Web www.innscotland.com

Located on the edge of the pretty village of Drymen, the Buchanan Arms is a popular hotel which offers snacks, lunches and dinners and good accommodation. This is the sort of place that is very well suited to family gatherings where there is likely to be something for all ages and tastes.

DUFFTOWN

A Taste of Speyside Restaurant
10 Balvenie Street, Dufftown
Banffshire AB55 4AB
Tel 01340 820860
email taste.speyside@nest.org.uk

Web www.scottish-info.com/scotland/
speyside.htm

A Taste of Speyside Restaurant has been offering a highly enjoyable experience to its customers for many years now. The cooking is wholesome, Scottish and very good and much reflects the speciality of the region – malt whisky!

DUMFRIES

Abbey Cottage
26 Main Street, New Abbey
Dumfries DG2 8BY
Tel 01387 850377
Fax 01848 200536

Abbey Cottage is a wonderful, family-run tearoom which only offers the very best home baking, snacks and light lunches. The hospitality is warm and genuine in cosy surroundings. There is also a good local craft gift shop to tempt you.

DUMFRIES

Reivers Restaurant
Cairndale Hotel & Leisure Club
English Street
Dumfries DG1 2DF
Tel 01387 254111
Fax 01387 250555
email suzanne@cairndalehotel.co.uk
Web www.cairndalehotel.co.uk

Cairndale is a large, privately-owned hotel situated close to the centre of the town. The hotel has good facilities and offers a consistent standard of traditional Scottish hospitality and cooking.

DUNBAR

Springfield Guest House
Belhaven Road, Dunbar
East Lothian EH42 1NH
Tel 01368 862502
Fax 01368 862 502
email smeed@tesco.net

Springfield Guest House is a small,

family run establishment which offers a relaxed atmosphere and comfortable surroundings. The food served here is good home cooking, using fresh, local ingredients which are simply prepared and presented.

Rokeby House
Doune Road
Dunblane
FK15 9AT
Tel 01786 824447
Fax 01786 821399
email rokeby.house@btconnect.com
Web www.aboutscotland.com/stirling/rokeby.html

Rokeby House is a delightful Edwardian building, tastefully renovated by its owners. This is a very high quality establishment where guests can enjoy excellent cooking with a contemporary twist, beautifully presented.

Jute Café Bar
Dundee Contemporary Arts
152 Nethergate
Dundee
DD1 4DY
Tel 01382 909235
Fax 01382 909221
email jutecafebar@hotmail.com
Web www.jutecafebar.co.uk

Jute Café Bar is open all day and is well worth visiting when taking in the arts. Surroundings are spacious and food is served all day. Cooking is contemporary and freshly cooked and the standard is very good.

The Fisherman's Tavern Hotel
10-16 Fort Street, Broughty Ferry
Dundee DD5 2AD
Tel 01382 775941
Fax 01382 477466
email bookings@fishermans.sol.co.uk
Web www.fishermans-tavern-hotel.co.uk

This is a typical Scottish pub located in a listed 17th Century fisherman's cottage. The service is friendly and the food is good Scottish pub fare.

Davaar House Hotel and Restaurant
126 Grieve Street
Dunfermline KY12 8DW
Tel 01383 721886
Fax 01383 623633

Davaar House is a family-run hotel and restaurant in a beautiful detached villa in a quiet street. The welcome is warm, menus are imaginative and cooking is skilled using the best local ingredients.

Garvock House Hotel
St John's Drive, Dunfermline KY12 7TU
Tel 01383 621067
Fax 01383 621168
email sales@garvock.co.uk
Web www.garvock.co.uk

Garvock House is a beautiful Georgian house, family-owned and run, in a private setting. Popular with locals and visitors, it offers good standards of service, personal attention, good menus and skilled cooking.

DUNKELD

The Pend
5 Brae Street
Dunkeld
Perthshire PH8 0BA
Tel 01350 727586
Fax 01350 727173
email molly@thepend.sol.co.uk
Web www.thepend.com

The Pend is a comfortable family home. Run by Marina, an accomplished host, this is an experience which lovers of good food won't want to miss. From breakfast to dinner, the cooking and standards are superb.

DUNKELD

The Royal Dunkeld Hotel
Atholl Street
Dunkeld
Perthshire PH8 0AR
Tel 01350 727322
Fax 01350 728989
email reservations@royaldunkeld.co.uk
Web www.royaldunkeld.co.uk/
www.royaldunkeldhotel.co.uk

The Royal Dunkeld is a traditional hotel located in the main street through Dunkeld. There is the option of informal dining in the bar where the food is simple but freshly prepared or more formal in the restaurant.

BY DUNKELD

Kinnaird
Kinnaird Estate
Dalguise, by Dunkeld, Perthshire
Tel 01796 482440

Kinnaird House is a country house which offers a very high standard of comfort and service. It is justifiably popular as the combination of surroundings and seriously excellent food make for a memorable experience.

DUNOON

Abbot's Brae Hotel
West Bay, Dunoon
Argyll PA23 7QJ
Tel 01369 705021
Fax 01369 701191
email info@abbotsbrae.co.uk
Web www.abbotsbrae.co.uk

Abbot's Brae Hotel is a beautiful house which is both comfortable and welcoming. The restaurant looks out onto sea views and the menus here are classic Scottish, cooked simply but to a very high standard. The Scottish Hotels of the Year Awards. STB 4 Star Small Hotel.

DUNOON

The Anchorage Hotel & Restaurant
Sandbank, By Dunoon
Argyll PA23 8QG
Tel 01369 705108
Fax 01369 705108
email long@anchorage.co.uk
Web www.anchorage.co.uk

This is a small intimate restaurant which looks directly onto the harbour.

The cooking uses fresh local produce prepared in a simple classic style with daily changing specials.

DUNOON

Chatters Restaurant
58 John Street
Dunoon
Argyll PA23 8BJ
Tel 01369 706402
email oldmill@cwcom.net
Web www.oldmill.mcmail.com/chatters

Rosemary MacInnes has been welcoming guests to Chatters for many years now and has been justifiably recognised for the high standards she has maintained. It is a warm, friendly restaurant where the emphasis is on good Scottish produce, prepared and presented with an assured touch.

DUNOON

Enmore Hotel
Dunoon
PA23 8HH
Tel 01369 702230
Fax 01369 702148
email enmorehotel@btinternet.com
Web www.enmorehotel.co.uk

Angela and David Wilson have owned and run the Enmore for many years. Today it remains a place where the high standard of welcome and cooking reinforces its reputation as one of Scotland's special destinations.

DUNURE

The Anchorage
Harbour View
Dunure KA7 4LN
Tel 01292 500295
Fax 01292 500432
email ashmegson@aol.com

Situated on the shores of the Holy Loch, the Anchorage Hotel is a charming Victorian house with welcoming and attentive hosts. The three-course menu is set in advance, taking into account guests' preferences, and offers traditional Scottish foods with modern flair.

EAST LINTON

Kippielaw Farmhouse
East Linton
East Lothian
EH41 4PY
Tel 01620 860368
Fax 01620 860368
email info@kippielawfarmhouse.co.uk
Web www.kippielawfarmhouse.co.uk

Kippielaw is a tastefully converted farmhouse in a beautiful setting. The welcome from the hosts is sincere and warm, a reflection of all-round high standards of hospitality – and that includes the meals which are expertly prepared and presented.

EDINBURGH

A Room In The Town
18 Howe Street
Edinburgh
EH3 6TG
Tel 0131 225 8204
Fax 0131 225 8204
Web www.aroomin.co.uk/thetown

A Room in the Town proves that it is possible to provide consistently high standards, even when the budget is restricted. A gem.

EDINBURGH

A Room In The West End
26 William Street
Edinburgh
EH3 7NH
Tel 0131 226 1036
Fax 0131 226 1036
Web www.aroomin.co.uk/thewestend

A Room in the West End adheres to the same policy that it is possible to produce consistently high standards day in and day out. No mean feat!

EDINBURGH

Amber
The Scotch Whisky Heritage Centre
354 Castlehill, The Royal Mile
Edinburgh EH1 2NE
Tel 0131 477 8477
Fax 0131 220 6288
email info@amber-restaurant.co.uk
Web www.amber-restaurant.co.uk

Located within the fascinating Scotch
Whisky Heritage Centre, Amber has
been recently renovated. It's a fine place
to enjoy a wide range of wholesome
Scottish fare in unique surroundings.

EDINBURGH

Appetite @ Rowlands
Howe Street
Edinburgh EH3 6LB
Tel 0131 225 3711
Fax 0131 225 3711

This superb takeaway and outside
catering business is located at the foot
of Howe Street in the New Town and is
a worthy entrant to this Guide. The
quality and freshness of the dishes
which are available both from the shop
and for outside catering is unquestioned.
They also have a superb range of quality
food items to stock up the home larder
and also sell a good range of wines.

EDINBURGH

The Atrium
Cambridge Street
Edinburgh
Tel 0131 228 8882
Fax 0131 228 8808
email eat@atriumrestaurant.co.uk
Web www.atriumrestaurant.co.uk

Andrew and Lisa Radford have been
running The Atrium for 12 years and in
that time it has consistently retained –
and built on – its reputation as one of
the best places to dine in Edinburgh. The
cooking here is highly skilled and uses
the best of local produce with a sense of
innovation and panache. Justifiably
popular, this is quite simply one of those
very special places. 2 AA Rosettes.
Michelin Bib Gourmande.Best Restaurant
in Edinburgh 2003/4 – The List.

EDINBURGH

Baxters at Ocean Terminal
Leith, Edinburgh
Tel 0131 553 0840
Web www.baxters.com
Hamper Freephone: 0800 1868 00

This high quality retail and dining outlet
is stylishly laid out over two floors. You
can select from a superb range of
quality food and other Scottish items –

something here for everyone. The Restaurant enjoys superb views of the Forth and Bridges and the menus offer simple, well prepared and presented Scottish food served by accomplished and friendly staff.

EDINBURGH

Bellini Restaurant
8b Abercromby Place
Edinburgh EH3 6LB
Tel 0131 476 2602
Fax 0131 476 2607

The food at Bellini, which is centrally located in the New Town, is in the classic Italian style, skilfully prepared by a chef who clearly enjoys what he does and has the confidence to present imaginative and colourful dishes.

EDINBURGH

Beluga Bar & Canteen Restaurant
30A Chambers Street
Edinburgh
EH1 1HU
Tel 0131 624 4545
Fax 0131 624 4546
Web www.beluga-edinburgh.com

Beluga is an elegant, modern restaurant offering skilled cooking which takes its influences from all corners of the world and marries them with high quality produce. This is an innovative and creative restaurant offering a high standard of service and food.

EDINBURGH

Best Western Edinburgh City Hotel
79 Lauriston Place
Edinburgh
EH3 9HZ
Tel 0131 622 7979
Fax 0131 622 7900
email reservations@
bestwesternedinburghcity.co.uk
Web www.bestwesternedinburghcity.co.uk

Built in 1879, this now privately

owned hotel was once the original Memorial Hospital dedicated to Sir James Young Simpson, discoverer of chloroform. To visit now, you'll find a contemporary dining room offering a menu of modern Scottish cooking, skilfully prepared in an innovative style.

EDINBURGH

Blue Bar Café
10 Cambridge Street
Edinburgh
EH1 2ED
Tel 0131 221 1222
Fax 0131 228 8808
email eat@bluebarcafe.com
Web www.bluebarcafe.com

Established in 1997, Blue Bar Café is run by Andrew and Lisa Radford and remains one of the most stylish cafés in Edinburgh. Its continuing popularity is based on a combination of good food, well served in an informal setting – and it's also a favourite for families. 1 AA Rosette

EDINBURGH

Britannia Spice
150 Commercial Street
Leith
Edinburgh
Tel 0131 555 2255

Arguably one of the best Indian Restaurants in Edinburgh, Britannia Spice offers a wide-ranging menu with something to offer all who enjoy classic and modern Indian food.

EDINBURGH

Potting Shed Restaurant
Bruntsfield Hotel
69 Bruntsfield Place
Edinburgh
EH10 4HH
Tel 0131 229 1393
Fax 0131 229 5634
email sales@thebruntsfield.co.uk
Web www.thebruntsfield.co.uk

The Potting Shed at the Bruntsfield
Hotel is a popular place on the South
side of the city. The food is Scottish and
colourfully and innovatively prepared
and presented by skilled chefs.

EDINBURGH

Café d'Odile
13 Randolph Crescent
Edinburgh
Tel 0131 225 5366

Café d'Odile is itself something of an
institution within the French Institute
and is deservedly popular with all who
enjoy good French cooking. It is only
open for lunch – although it can be
booked privately for parties for dinner.
It is simple, unpretentious and good
value in pleasant surroundings.

EDINBURGH

Café Hub
Castlehill
Royal Mile
Edinburgh
EH1 2NE
Tel 0131 473 2067
Fax 0131 473 2016
email thehub@eif.co.uk
Web www.eif.co.uk/thehub

The Hub, situated at the top of
Castlehill, is a popular casual meeting
place which offers a range of stylish
meals all day. The food served here is
innovative and stylish to match the
contemporary clientele it attracts.

EDINBURGH

Café Marlayne
76 Thistle Street
Edinburgh
Tel 0131 226 2230

Café Marlayne is a tiny, intimate
restaurant which serves superb French
food, unpretentious but quite simply
very good!

EDINBURGH

Caledonian Hilton Hotel
Princes Street
Edinburgh
EH1 2AB

Affectionately known locally as the
Caley, this is an Edinburgh landmark in
a stunning location. As you would
expect from a top class hotel, there is a
range of dining options here and the
cooking is first rate, whether served in
informal or more formal surroundings.

EDINBURGH

Centotre
103 George Street
Edinburgh
EH2 3ES
Tel 0131 225 1550
Web www.centotre.com

Centotre (Italian for 103) is one of
the newest additions to the Edinburgh
culinary scene. It is primarily a bistro
restaurant where you can enjoy a
glass of excellent wine at the bar, or
take a table for a light meal or a
more substantial one. Authentic
Italian – the quality is superb and the
hosts are on hand to ensure you
enjoy the experience. Deservedly
popular.

EDINBURGH

Channings Restaurant
15 South Learmonth Gardens
Edinburgh
EH4 1EZ
Tel 0131 315 2225
Fax 0131 332 9631
email restaurant@channings.co.uk
Web www.channings.co.uk

Located in a primarily residential area, Channings is a popular hotel with a bar and restaurants. It's a very well run and welcoming venue, offering extremely good food in Channings Restaurant, the more formal of the two dining options.

EDINBURGH

Bacchus
Christopher North House Hotel
6 Gloucester Place
Edinburgh
EH3 6EF
Tel 0131 225 2720
Fax 0131 220 4706
email sales@christophernorth.co.uk
Web www.christophernorth.co.uk

Christopher North House is an elegant house in Edinburgh's New Town. The restaurant is tastefully decorated and the cooking is good, modern and served in a relaxed style.

EDINBURGH

Circus Café
Royal Circus
Edinburgh
Tel 0131 220 0333

Circus Café has become 'the' place in Stockbridge to meet for coffee, lunch, a drink or dinner. It is comfortable and contemporary and the menus have something to suit everyone with very friendly and knowledgeable staff. Don't miss out on the great deli downstairs!

EDINBURGH

Cosmo Restaurant
58A North Castle Street
Edinburgh
EH2 3LU
Tel 0131 226 6743
Fax 0131 226 6743
email cosmos@tiscali.co.uk
Web www.cosmo-restaurant.co.uk

Cosmo's has long been an Edinburgh tradition with its stylish mix of Italian and Scottish dishes skilfully prepared and presented. The high standards here ensure you'll enjoy your visit.

EDINBURGH

Daniel's Bistro
88 Commercial Street
Leith
Edinburgh EH3 6SF

Located in Edinburgh's rapidly developing waterfront in Leith, this stylish Bistro is a friendly and relaxed place to enjoy the highly distinctive French menu. The standard of cooking and service is superb and the welcome enthusiastic.

EDINBURGH

David Bann's
St Mary's Street
Edinburgh
Tel 0131 556 5888

This is a fine Vegetarian Restaurant with a growing reputation for defying – in the nicest possible way – the view that a meal is incomplete without meat. In fact, the cooking here is skilled and innovative and the whole experience is most enjoyable.

EDINBURGH

The Doric Tavern
15/16 Market Street
Edinburgh EH1 1DE
Tel 0131 225 1084
Fax 0131 220 0894
email info@mowco.co.uk
Web www.thedoric.co.uk

The Doric Tavern is a friendly, popular
wine bar whose menus change often
depending upon the availability of fresh
produce. The food is Scottish with
European influences, complemented
with an excellent selection of wines.

EDINBURGH

Dubh Prais
123b High Street
Edinburgh EH1 1SG
Tel 0131 557 5732
Fax 0131 557 5263

Dubh Prais is the place on Edinburgh's
High Street where James and Heather
McWilliams have established a wonderful
reputation. This small restaurant is cosy
and intimate and the cooking is highly
skilled using only the very best Scottish
produce served in contemporary style.

EDINBURGH

Duck's at Le Marché Noir
2/4 Eyre Place
Edinburgh EH3 5EP
Tel 0131 558 1608
Fax 0131 556 0798
email bookings@ducks.co.uk
Web www.ducks.co.uk

This is a stylish New Town restaurant
hosted by proprietor Malcolm Duck.
The atmosphere here is intimate and
the cooking is superb – excellent
Scottish produce is prepared and
presented in French style. Look out for
the rather special wine list to find
something to complement your
meal.

EDINBURGH

First Coast
99 Dalry Road
Edinburgh
Tel 0131 313 4404

First Coast is fast developing a name for
itself as one of the 'don't-miss' places
to dine in Edinburgh. It's a stylish and
welcoming restaurant serving very
good food, simply prepared and
presented.

EDINBURGH

Fishers
The Shore
Leith
Edinburgh
Tel 0131 554 5666

An extremely popular restaurant,
Fishers has long had an enviable
reputation as one of the best places in
Edinburgh to enjoy seafood. The
cooking is simple, highly proficient and
uses imaginative twists to complement
the very best produce.

EDINBURGH

Fishers in the City
58 Thistle Street
Edinburgh
Tel 0131 225 5109

The sister restaurant to Fishers in Leith,
this is a more contemporary version of
the same. Excellent seafood, cooked
with thought and care with innovative
touches. Very busy, too, so be sure to
book.

Gallery of Modern Art Café
Belford Road
Edinburgh

A great meeting place which offers a fine selection of good value self-service dishes and is open all day. This is a particularly lovely place to sit on a warm day as the patio is sheltered. Tends to be popular with families and children.

Grain Store Restaurant
30 Victoria Street
Edinburgh
EH1 2JN
Tel 0131 225 7635
Fax 0131 622 7313
email contact@
grainstore-restaurant.co.uk
Web www.grainstore-restaurant.co.uk

The Grainstore is a very popular restaurant located in the delightful Victoria Street, which has a character all of its own. It is an informal, comfortable setting from which to enjoy superb cooking expertly prepared and presented.

Hadrian's Brasserie
The Balmoral Hotel,
1 Princes Street
Edinburgh
EH2 2EQ
Tel 0131 557 5000
Fax 0131 557 3747
Web www.rfhotels.com

Hadrians can be accessed either from The Balmoral Hotel or from the corner of North Bridge. It is a classic brasserie and is also rightly popular for its hearty Sunday brunch.

Haldanes Restaurant
39a Albany Street
Edinburgh EH1 3QY
Tel 0131 556 8407
Fax 0131 556 2662
email dinehaldanes@aol.com
Web www.haldanesrestaurant.com

Haldanes is owned and run by George and Michelle Kelso. Michelle is an accomplished and highly experienced hostess and George's skills as a Chef have long been recognised by his peers and customers. Haldanes is justifiably known for the consistently high standards it achieves and deserves its place amongst the best dining experiences in Edinburgh. Wine List of Excellence Award

The Hallion Club
12 Picardy Place
Edinburgh EH1 3JT
Tel 0131 523 1523

The Hallion Club is only open to members, but is worth a mention here as it offers a superb culinary experience in its dining room and lots of fun in its trendy and popular bar.

Henderson's Salad Table
94 Hanover Street
Edinburgh EH2 1DR
Tel 0131 225 2131
Fax 0131 220 3542
email mail@
hendersonsofedinburgh.co.uk

Web www.hendersonsofedinburgh.co.uk

Henderson's is another Edinburgh institution, having served good wholesome vegetarian cooking for more than 40 years. It is still family run and is open all day providing a good standard of meals and snacks, with many imaginative touches.

EDINBURGH

Howies Stockbridge
4-6 Glanville Place
Edinburgh EH3 6SZ
email howiesuk@hotmail.com

A popular, modern bistro, Howies in Stockbridge is owned by David Scott. This restaurant serves an excellent standard of Scottish cooking served in a contemporary style to match the surroundings.

EDINBURGH

Igg's Restaurant
15 Jeffrey Street
Edinburgh EH1 1DR
Tel 0131 557 8184
Fax 0131 652 3774

Igg's is a well-established, stylish eatery where Spain meets Scotland with aplomb. Owner-run, Igg's is friendly and the service is attentive. The food here is a successful blend of contemporary Scottish with a strong Spanish influence.

EDINBURGH

Jackson's Restaurant
209 High Street, Royal Mile
Edinburgh EH1 1PE
Tel 0131 225 1793
Fax 0131 2200620

Jackson's is an interesting small restaurant in an ideal location for those exploring the Old Town of Edinburgh. It is friendly and comfortable and serves good Scottish cooking with a contemporary flavour.

EDINBURGH

Keepers Restaurant
13B Dundas Street
Edinburgh EH3 6QG
Tel 0131 556 5707
Fax 0131 556 5707
email keepers.restaurant@virgin.net
Web www.keepersrestaurant.co.uk

Keepers, run by Keith and Marie Cowie, is a delightful cellar restaurant which is intimate and cosy. While game is a speciality, many other dishes are also prepared with skill in a traditional fashion with innovative touches.

EDINBURGH

Kweilin
19 Dundas Street
Edinburgh
Tel 0131 557 1875

Another personal favourite, The Kweilin has been serving excellent Chinese food here for years. It is a traditional styled Chinese Restaurant which offers excellent quality food and good service.

EDINBURGH

L'Alba D'Oro
5 Henderson Row
Edinburgh EH3 5DH
Tel 0131 557 2580
Fax 0131 557 2580

For really good quality fish and chips in Edinburgh's New Town, look no further than L'Alba d'Oro. This family-run Italian business offers a huge range of dishes in addition to the traditional ones. One of the best of its kind.

EDINBURGH

La Garrigue
31 Jeffrey Street
Edinburgh
EH1 1DH
Tel 0131 557 3032
Fax 0131 557 3032

Jean Michel is a wonderfully skilled Chef and for those who really enjoy good food, particularly with a French influence, you could do no better than dine at La Garrigue. Dishes are typical of La Garrigue region whilst using the very best of Scottish ingredients. A real favourite.

EDINBURGH

La P'tite Folie
9 Randolph Place
Edinburgh
EH3 7TE
Tel 0131 225 8678
Fax 0131 225 6477
Web www.lafayette-restaurant.co.uk

Situated in the West End, this elegant restaurant is an excellent place to enjoy French cooking using good local ingredients. La P'tite Folie also offers a well-chosen wine list and the service is attentive and friendly.

EDINBURGH

Le Café Saint-Honoré
34 North West Thistle Street Lane
Edinburgh
EH2 1EA
Tel 0131 226 2211
Web www.cafesthonore.com

Le Café St Honore is a busy bistro restaurant where customers enjoy superior French cooking in traditional environs. It has been successfully run for years by Chris and Gill Colverson who have been rightly recognised for the consistent quality of this marvellous restaurant.

EDINBURGH

The Marque
19-21 Causewayside
Edinburgh EH9 1QF
Tel 0131 466 6660
Fax 0131 466 6661

The Marque is a superb restaurant run by Lara Kearney. This stylish establishment offers attentive service and a high standard of cooking which is both imaginative and innovative. And if you like this, you may also want to try Marque Central in Grindlay Street.

EDINBURGH

Pentland Restaurant
**Marriott Dalmahoy Hotel &
Country Club**
Kirknewton
Edinburgh EH27 8EB
Tel 0131 3334099
0131 3353518
email paul.bean@whitbread.com
Web www.marriot.com

Situated on the outskirts of Edinburgh, the Marriott Dalmahoy is a must for visiting golfers. This is a popular hotel with locals and visitors offering fine dining in the Pentland Restaurant which has magnificent views over the 18th hole with Edinburgh Castle in the background.

EDINBURGH

Martin's Restaurant
70 Rose Street North Lane
Edinburgh
EH2 3DX

Martin's Restaurant is centrally-located in a quiet lane just off Princes Street. It is a bit of an institution which has been run by Martin and Gay Irons for many years. The cooking here is of the highest standard, as is the service. Don't miss out on the wonderful cheeseboard and Martin's descriptions thereof!

EDINBURGH

No 3 Royal Terrace

3 Royal Terrace
Edinburgh
EH7 5AB
Tel 0131 477 4747
Fax 0131 477 4747
email nigel@howgate.f9.co.uk
Web www.howgate.f9.co.uk

No 3 Royal Terrace is owned by the same people who have the popular Howgate on the outskirts of the city. It is an elegant and comfortable restaurant which offers exciting menus of Scottish food cooked in a contemporary style.

EDINBURGH

No 27 Charlotte Square

27 Charlotte Square
Edinburgh
EH2 4ET
Tel 0131 243 9339
Fax 0131 243 9595
email catering@nts.org.uk
Web www.nts.org.uk

A great place to meet for coffee, home bakes or a light lunch. No 27 Charlotte Square is the jewel in the National Trust crown. It also has a good shop with a Scottish flavour.

EDINBURGH

Number One

The Balmoral Hotel
1 Princes Street
Edinburgh
EH2 2EQ
Tel 0131 557 6727
Fax 0131 557 8740

email numberone@ thebalmoralhotel.com
Web www.rfhotels.com

Part of The Balmoral Hotel – arguably the finest hotel in Edinburgh – this restaurant deserves its own entry as the standard it sets and delivers is consistently second to none. Jeff Bland is a superbly skilled Chef who has quite rightly long been admired for his achievements. This is fine dining at its best in a beautiful setting with superb service.

EDINBURGH

Ochre Vita

Channings Hotel
15 South Learmonth Gardens
Edinburgh EH4 1EZ
Tel 0131 315 2225
Fax 0131 332 9631

With views towards Fettes College, Channings is a popular hotel with a bar and restaurants. Ochre Vita is the more informal dining option at Channings. Menus are contemporary, cooking skilled and the atmosphere relaxed.

EDINBURGH

Oloroso

33 Castle Street, Edinburgh
Tel 0131 226 7614

Oloroso will always be remembered as the dream of Tony Singh and James Sankey. Sadly, we lost James all too soon, but Tony, a highly skilled chef, ensures it remains one of the best dining experiences in the city with certainly the best views! On a sunny day the Terrace is 'the' place to be.

Pret à Manger
54 Shandwick Place
Edinburgh EH2 4RT
Tel 0131 229 0097

The Pret à Manger chain of takeaways offer some of the highest standards achievable in this type of eatery. The sandwiches are all freshly made on the premises using only the finest ingredients with great innovation.

Restaurant At The Bonham
35 Drumsheugh Gardens
Edinburgh EH3 7RN
Tel 0131 623 9319
Fax 0131 226 6080
email restaurant@thebonham.com
Web www.thebonham.com

The Restaurant at The Bonham is a stylish venue in the city's West End. The property has been renovated in a contemporary style whilst retaining many original features. Menus are imaginative, changing regularly and the cooking is highly skilled. 4 Red Stars, Silver Green Tourism Award.

Restaurant Martin Wishart
The Shore
Leith
Edinburgh
Tel 0131 553 3557

Restaurant Martin Wishart boasts one of the most impressive dining experiences to be enjoyed in Scotland. Recently extended, it offers the highest standard of cooking and service in delightful surroundings. A meal here is a memorable event – but you'll need to book well in advance.

Rhubarb
Prestonfield House Hotel
Priestfield Road
Edinburgh
EH16 5UT
Tel 0131 225 0976
Fax 0131 668 3976
Web www.rhubarb-restaurant.com

Rhubarb is the new restaurant at Prestonfield Hotel, which has been extensively and luxuriously refurbished by new owner James Thomson. It takes its name from Prestonfield's reputation as having been the first Scottish estate to grow rhubarb! The food here is of the highest quality, served with style. Menus are Scottish with successful innovative twists. STB 5 Star Hotel.

Rogue
63 Morrison Street
Edinburgh
Tel 0131 228 2700

Rogue, tucked in a corner of the city's financial district, continues to be one of the best and most interesting eateries in Edinburgh. The food is simply superb, served in stylish surroundings under Dave Ramsden's well-disciplined supervision.

EDINBURGH

Santini
Conference Square
Edinburgh
Tel 0131 221 7788

Santini is located in Conference Square and is part of the Sheraton Spa (excellent). Both its formal and bistro sections offer a splendid selection of Italian food.

EDINBURGH

Sheraton Grand Hotel
1 Festival Square
Edinburgh
EH3 9SR

The Sheraton is a sophisticated hotel, luxuriously appointed and in an ideal central location. It has two restaurants – the Grill which offers fine dining and an exemplary standard of service and The Terrace which is more informal but still achieves very high quality.

EDINBURGH

Skerries Restaurant
Dunstane House
4 West Coates
Haymarket
Edinburgh
EH12 5JQ
Tel 0131 337 6169
Fax 0131 337 6060
email reservations@ dunstanehousehotel.co.uk
Web www.dunstanehousehotel.co.uk

Skerries is a small hotel with a splendid restaurant specialising in produce from Orkney and Shetland, including seafood and beef and lamb. The welcome is genuine and the setting is a subtle blend of Orcadian and Victorian.

EDINBURGH

Skippers
1a Dock Place
Edinburgh
Tel 0131 554 1018

Skippers is another excellent bistro in Leith which has a long-standing reputation for quality. The tang of the sea in the air adds to the atmosphere which is appropriate for the speciality – this is one of the best places to enjoy seafood in Edinburgh.

EDINBURGH

Stac Polly
29-33 Dublin Street
Edinburgh
EH3 6NL
Tel 0131 556 2231
Fax 0131 557 9779
Web www.stacpolly.co.uk

Stac Polly is a charming Scottish Restaurant set in a basement in the New Town. The menu is varied but specialises in Scottish dishes, all of which are skilfully prepared and presented. There is another Stac Polly in Grindlay Street which is equally good.

EDINBURGH

Stockbridge Restaurant
54 St Stephen Street
Edinburgh
EH3 5AL
Tel 0131 226 6766

Stockbridge Restaurant is now under new ownership. It is located in the delightful St Stephen Street which is well known for its antique and second-hand shops. This restaurant offers a very high standard of cooking with interesting and innovative menus.

EDINBURGH

Tower Restaurant & Terrace
Museum of Scotland
Chambers Street
Edinburgh
EH1 1JF
Tel 0131 225 3003
Fax 0131 220 4392
email reservations@
tower-restaurant.com
Web www.tower-restaurant.com

The Tower is located at the top of the Museum of Scotland in Chambers Street and has some of the most impressive views of the city. This is a stylish, modern restaurant which serves food of a very high quality, presented in straightfoward, contemporary style.

EDINBURGH

Valvona & Crolla
19 Elm Row
Edinburgh
EH7 4AA
Tel 0131 556 6066
Fax 0131 556 1668
email sales@valvonacrolla.co.uk
Web www.valvonacrolla.co.uk

Valvona and Crolla is an Edinburgh institution where you can find an enormous array of some of the best Italian delicacies and staples. If you are not sure what you need the staff are knowledgeable and friendly. There is also an excellent cafe/bar where you can enjoy some of the delights here on site.

EDINBURGH

The Witchery by the Castle
Castlehill, The Royal Mile
Edinburgh EH1 2NF
Tel 0131 225 5613
Fax 0131 220 4392
email reservations@thewitchery.com
Web www.thewitchery.com

The Witchery is known, and deservedly so, as one of the finest and most atmospheric restaurants in Edinburgh. You can enjoy the very best of Scottish cooking, imaginatively prepared and served with style and aplomb. Watch out for James Thomson's splendid wine list!

EDINBURGH

Yo Sushi
66 Rose Street
Edinburgh
Tel 0131 220 6040

Those who enjoy Japanese food will be aware of the Yo Sushi experience. Sitting at the bar whilst watching the chefs prepare the dishes is an experience in itself. Not for the faint-hearted, perhaps, but if you like Japanese food you will enjoy this informal approach. Downstairs – adults only – there is another take on the Japanese dining experience.

EDINBURGH

Yumi
2 Wester Coates
Edinburgh
Tel 0131 337 2173

This is a unique Japanese Restaurant set within a splendid Victorian house. Here the staff are in kimonos and the food is authentic Japanese – a real delight. Its popularity with Japanese visitors is a testament to its quality and authenticity.

ELGIN

The Mansefield Hotel
2 Mayne Road
Elgin IV30 1NY
Tel 01343 540883
Fax 01343 552491
email reception@themansefield.com
Web www.themansefield.com

The Mansefield Hotel is situated close to the town centre and is an extremely well appointed, refurbished former manse. It is an ideal place to stay and/or dine; the rooms are comfortable and the menus are classic Scottish using good locally-sourced ingredients.

ELIE

Sangsters
51 High Street, Elie
Fife KY9 1BZ
Tel 01333 330374
Fax 01333 330364

Bruce Sangster makes a welcome return to Scotland at this intimate restaurant in Elie. A highly skilled and experienced Chef, his cooking is superb and uses only the very best local ingredients. Well worth experiencing the very best that this chef can offer.

ELIE

The Ship Inn
The Toft, Elie
Tel 01333 330246

The Ship Inn has been an institution in Elie for many years. Whether for a drink in the courtyard opposite, a quick bar meal or dining upstairs, where the views are superb, this is a key meeting place in Elie, popular with residents and visitors alike. Food is good and portions generous.

ELLON

Haddo House
Tarves
Ellon
Aberdeenshire
AB41 7EQ
Tel 01651 851440
Fax 01651 851888
email haddo@nts.org.uk
Web www.nts.org.uk

Haddo House is another notable National Trust property which sits in wonderful surroundings. The restaurant offers a range of delicious home baking, light snacks and lunches and the staff are friendly and welcoming.

EVANTON

Visitor Centre – Storehouse of Foulis
Foulis Ferry
Evanton
Ross & Cromarty
IV16 9UX
Tel 01349 830000
Fax 01349 830033
email restaurant@
storehouseoffoulis.co.uk
Web www.storehouseoffoulis.co.uk

This is a unique Highland Visitor Attraction which sits on the delightful Cromarty Firth. The tearoom is open all day and offers a very good range of home baking, light snacks and lunches in spacious surroundings.

FAIRLIE

Fin's Seafood Restaurant
Fencefoot
Fairlie
Ayrshire
KA29 OEG
email fencebay@aol.com

Fins Seafood Restaurant is a great place to sample an exceptional range of the freshest seafood in congenial surroundings. The fish is cooked with flair and a light touch.

FALKLAND

The Greenhouse Restaurant
High Street, Falkland
Fife KY15 7BU
Tel 01337 858400
Fax 01337 858400
email q_dalrymple@yahoo.co.uk
Web www.thegreenhouserestaurant.com

Falkland is a delightful, pretty Fife village which has been popular with visitors to its magnificent Palace for many a year. The Greenhouse Restaurant is a bistro-style establishment with an informal and stylish atmosphere. The cooking here is skilled and great care is taken with the best local and organic ingredients.

FALKLAND

The Hayloft Tearoom
Back Wynd, Falkland
Fife KY15 7BX
Tel 01337 857590
email haylofttrm@aol.com

The Hayloft is a traditional Scottish tearoom, located in a traditional terraced cottage, and is renowned for offering a wide range of very tasty home baking, preserves and light snacks.

FEARN

Glenmorangie – The Highland Home at Cadboll
Cadboll, Fearn
by Tain IV20 1XP
Tel 01862 871671
Fax 01862 871625
email relax@glenmorangie.co.uk
Web www.glenmorangie.com

Glenmorangie is a fine country house in a lovely setting which offers comfort and style in this beautiful part of Scotland. The menus here are carefully composed to make good use of local produce and incorporate only the finest locally-sourced and grown ingredients.

FINTRY

Culcreuch Castle
Castle Bar, Fintry
Stirlingshire G63 0LW
Tel 01360 860555
Fax 01360 860556
email info@culcreuch.com
Web www.culcreuch.com

Culcreuch Castle is an interesting setting from which to enjoy good bar meals. The house has been renovated whilst retaining its historical feel. The menus here are extensive, cooking is unpretentious and the ambience is informal.

FOCHABERS

Baxters Highland Village
Fochabers
Moray IV32 7LD
Tel 01343 820666
Fax 01343 821790
email highland.village@baxters.co.uk
Web www.baxters.co.uk

Baxters Highland Village is a fascinating place to visit. This is a high quality visitor attraction with something to offer everyone, from shopping to eating. The restaurant is self service and the food is good Scottish – and that includes value for money!

FORFAR

The Chapelbank House Hotel & Restaurant
69 East High Street, Forfar
Angus DD8 2EP
Tel 01307 463151
Fax 01307 461922

email agun@btconnect.com
Web www.chapelbank.com

Chapelbank House Hotel and Restaurant is a small hotel in the centre of the town of Forfar. It is an attractive Victorian house where guests can relax and make the most of a highly enjoyable dining experience in a comfortable setting.

FORRES

Brodie Castle
Brodie, Forres
Moray IV36 2TE
Tel 01309 641371
Fax 01309 641600
email fdingwall@nts.org.uk
Web www.nts.org.uk

Brodie Castle is another fine National Trust property, located in its own beautiful grounds. The tearoom offers a delectable range of home baking, light snacks and some interesting blackboard specials for those with an appetite for something more substantial.

FORRES

Knockomie Hotel
Grantown Road, Forres
Moray IV36 2SG
Tel 01309 673146
Fax 01309 673290
email stay@knockomie.co.uk
Web www.knockomie.co.uk

A family-run hotel situated on the outskirts of the town, Knockomie Hotel has both a bistro, which offers a wide range of dishes, and a more formal dining room. In both cases, the cooking here uses only the best locally-sourced produce, deftly prepared and attractively presented.

FORRES

Ramnee Hotel
Hamblins Dining Room
Victoria Road

Forres
Moray IV36 3BN
Tel 01309 672410
Fax 01309 673392
email ramneehotel@btconnect.com
Web www.ramneehotel.net

Ramnee Hotel is an Edwardian mansion situated in a prime location in Forres. There is something for everyone here, from light meals to a memorable dining experience in the Dining Room. The cooking is distinguished and makes good use of local produce prepared by an accomplished team.

FORT WILLIAM

Allt-nan-Ros Hotel
Onich
Fort William
Inverness-shire
PH33 6RY
Tel 01855 821210
Fax 01855 821462
email reception@allt-nan-ros.co.uk
Web www.allt-nan-ros.co.uk

Allt-Nan-Ros is a good, comfortable hotel run by attenative and accomplished hosts. The cooking here is of a high standard, prepared and presented by chefs who clearly have great enthusiasm for the produce they work with.

FORT WILLIAM

Crannog Restaurant
Town Pier
Fort William PH33 7PT
Tel 01397 703919
Fax 01397 705026
email finlayfin@btiopenworld.com
Web www.crannog.net

Crannog is an excellent example of the kind of treats you can expect when fish is prepared by people who also catch it! The restaurant is uniquely situated on Loch Linnhe and is a fine place to enjoy an exceptional meal.

FORT WILLIAM

Inverlochy Castle
Torlundy
Fort William PH33 6SN
Tel 01397 702177

Inverlochy Castle is simply one of the most special places to stay in Scotland. It is a grand property with luxurious accommodation and the highest of standards in service and surroundings. As you would expect, the cooking, shares these high standards. Skilful, carefully composed menus and the best produce ensure a memorable experience.

FORT WILLIAM

The Moorings Hotel
Banavie
Fort William
PH33 7LY
Tel 01397 772797
Fax 01397 772441
email reservations@
mooringsfortwilliam.co.uk
Web www.moorings-fortwilliam.co.uk

The Moorings, living up to its name, is situated on the banks of the Caledonian Canal. Menus are often adventurous and offer a range of dishes to suit all appetites. The restaurant is particularly comfortable and welcoming.

FORT WILLIAM

No 4 Cameron Square
Cameron Square
Fort William
Inverness-shire
PH33 6AJ
Tel 01397 704222
Fax 01397 704448
Web www.no4-fortwilliam.co.uk

Just off Fort William's High Street, No. 4 is a pleasant small restaurant which offers an extensive range of well-cooked snacks, light lunches and elegant dinners.

FORTROSE

Cathedral Restaurant
Anderson Hotel
Union Street
Fortrose
IV10 8TD
Tel 01381 620236
Fax 01381 620236
email info@theanderson.co.uk
Web www.fortrosehotel.co.uk

Anderson Hotel is family-run and is ideally located for exploring the area. The chefs make particularly good use of local produce in the bar with daily specials. Something for everyone.

GAIRLOCH

Badachro Inn
Badachro
Gairloch
Ross-shire IV21 2AA
Tel 01445 741255
Fax 01445 741319
email martyn@badachroinn.com
Web www.badachroinn.com

The Badachro Inn is in a lovely situation on the seashore by Gairloch. The food is of a good standard using locally-landed seafood and produce. A beautiful location to enjoy good food.

GAIRLOCH

The Creel
Charleston House
Gairloch
Ross-shire
IV21 2AH
Tel 01445 712497
Fax 01445 712688
email morag@charlestonhouse.co.uk
Web www.charlestonhouse.co.uk

The Creel is a most attractive restaurant with rooms where proprietors offer a good standard of Scottish cooking. As the name would suggest the emphasis is on local seafood, carefully cooked with innovative touches.

GATTONSIDE

Chapters Bistro
Main Street
Gattonside
TD6 9NB
Tel 01896 823217

This is a superb bistro where you are assured good service, relaxing ambience and excellent food. Menus reflect the high standard of local produce available and the cooking is highly skilled and contemporary.

GLAMIS

Castleton House Hotel
by Glamis
Angus
DD8 1SJ
Tel 01307 840340
Fax 01307 840506
email hotel@castletonglamis.co.uk
Web www.castletonglamis.co.uk

Castleton House Hotel is one of the best small hotels in the area offering a very high standard of accommodation and food, all of which is locally sourced and prepared with skill and flair.

GLASGOW

Arthouse Hotel
129 Bath Street
Glasgow
G2 2SZ
Tel 0141 221 6789
Fax 0141 221 6777
email info@arthousehotel.com
Web www.arthousehotel.com

The Arthouse Hotel is home to the Arthouse Grill which is a popular restaurant in this central location. The hotel itself is superb, offering a very high standard of accommodation. The restaurant matches those standards in the food it serves in comfortable surroundings.

GLASGOW

Babbity Bowster
16-18 Blackfriars Street
Glasgow G1 1PE
Tel 0141 552 5055
Fax 0141 552 7774
email babbitybowster@gofornet.co.uk

Babbity Bowster is a friendly and comfortable hotel in Glasgow and is popular venue for locals and visitors. The bar is lively, the food in the restaurant is of exceptional quality. Excellent local produce skilfully prepared and imaginatively presented.

GLASGOW

Brian Maule at the Chardon d'Or
176 West Regent Street
Glasgow
Tel 0141 248 3801

The Chardon d'Or is another of Scotland's finest restaurants with Brian Maule at the helm in the kitchen – a highly proficient and passionate Chef. The cooking here is simply superb. There is a French influence in the origins whilst only the best produce is carefully and skilfully prepared and presented. Excellent service front-of-house completes the experience.

GLASGOW

The Buttery
652 Argyle Street
Glasgow
G3 8UF
Tel 0141 221 8188
Fax 0141 204 4639

Willie Deans is another of Scotland's top Chefs who makes cooking an art. The Buttery has re-established itself as one of Glasgow's top eateries. Always a classic, the food and service here are of the highest standard. Well worth experiencing to fully appreciate all that a highly-skilled Chef can offer.

GLASGOW

Café Gandolfi
64 Albion Street
Glasgow
G1 1NY
Tel 0141 552 6813

Café Gandolfi is run by Seamus
MacInnes and has been an institution in
Glasgow for many years – and
justifiably so. This is a casual place
where good local food is served all day
in stylish surroundings.

GLASGOW

Café Ostra
15 John St
Glasgow
G1 1HP
Tel 0141 552 4433
Web www.cafeostra.com

Café Ostra is the new informal
seafood restaurant owned by Alan
Tomkins (Gamba and Papingo also)
and is fast becoming a hit with
Glaswegians. A good place to enjoy
contemporary menus, excellent
cooking in the light airy surroundings
of the Italian Centre.

GLASGOW

City Merchant Restaurant
97 Candleriggs
Glasgow
G1 1NP
Tel 0141 553 1577
Fax 0141 553 1588
email citymerchant@btinternet.com
Web www.citymerchant.co.uk

City Merchant is a warm, welcoming
restaurant in the Merchant City, run by
Tony and Linda Matteo. This is a
popular venue which offers a very high
standard of menus and cooking using
the finest local produce.

GLASGOW

Gamba
225a West George Street, Glasgow
Tel 0141 572 0899
email info@gamba.co.uk
Web www.gamba.co.uk

Gamba is a 'must visit' for lovers of
seafood; very popular, seriously well run
and where the cooking is consistently
excellent and innovative. Winner – 'Best
Glasgow Restaurant' 2003-2004 The List.

GLASGOW

Camerons
Hilton Glasgow
1 William Street
Glasgow G3 8HT
Tel 0141 204 5555
Fax 0141 204 5004
email matthew.mullan@hilton.com
Web www.hilton.com

The Hilton Hotel is fortunate to have
one of the top Chefs in Scotland. In
Camerons, the more formal restaurant,
there are interesting and intriguing
menus, the cooking is highly skilled
and service is excellent. Minskys is less
formal and offers a relaxed buffet style.

GLASGOW

The Inn on the Green
25 Greenhead Street
Glasgow G40 1ES
Tel 0141 554 0165
Fax 0141 556 4678
email sales@theinnonthegreen.co.uk
Web www.theinnonthegreen.co.uk

The Inn on the Green Hotel overlooks

Glasgow Green and is a congenial and welcoming restaurant. It is a popular venue where the informal surroundings blend well with modern Scottish cooking and good service. Live music often features in the evenings.

GLASGOW

La Bonne Auberge
Holiday Inn Hotel
161 West Nile Street
Glasgow G1 2RL
Tel 0141 352 8310
Fax 0141 332 7447
email triciafitzsimmons@higlasgow.com
Web www.higlasgow.com

La Bonne Auberge is a French bistro-style restaurant located within the Holiday Inn. It has a distinctly French feel to it but, while the menus are French in style, the dishes are made with good Scottish produce, cooked with skill and presented with care.

GLASGOW

Lux
1051 Great Western Road
Glasgow G12 0XP
Tel 0141 576 7576
Fax 0141 576 0162
email lux_stazione@gtwestern-rd.fsnet.co.uk
Web www.lux.5pm.co.uk

Lux is a stylish contemporary restaurant located in the popular West End of the city. The cooking is modern and innovative and uses quality Scottish produce to create dishes which are presented by friendly, welcoming staff.

GLASGOW

The Brasserie on George Square
Millennium Hotel
40 George Square
Glasgow
G2 1DS
Tel 0141 332 6711
Fax 0141 332 4264
email david.ibbotson@mill-cop.com
Web www.millenniumhotels.com

With great views of the bustling George Square, The Brasserie of the Millennium Hotel is a popular meeting place. Menus are in a contemporary Scottish style and the high standard of service and cooking complement each other well.

GLASGOW

Oko
68 Ingram Street
Glasgow
Tel 0141 572 1500

Oko is one of only a few Japanese eateries in Glasgow and is a good place to satisfy your passion for – or indeed your curiosity about – Japanese cuisine. It has the conveyor belt option and booths and the food is of a high standard.

GLASGOW

Papingo
104 Bath Street
Glasgow
Tel 0141 332 6678

Papingo is a seriously good bistro located in a basement in the city centre. It's easy to see why it's so popular, with a consistently high standard of food, cooking and service. Well worth a visit. Winner – 'Auchentoshan Spirit of Glasgow Awards' 2003.

GLASGOW

The Edwardian Kitchen Restaurant
Pollok House
Pollok Country Park
2060 Pollokshaws Road
Glasgow G43 1AT
Tel 0141 616 6410
Fax 0141 616 6521
email fmclean@nts.org.uk
Web www.nts.org.uk

Located within Pollok Estate, Pollok House is another National Trust property which is well worth a visit. The grounds and the house are beautiful and the Edwardian Kitchen Restaurant is a very pleasant place to enjoy a range of home baking, snacks and light lunches.

GLASGOW

Pret à Manger
69 Bothwell Street
Glasgow
G2 6TS
Tel 0141 221 2721

Fax 0141 221 3406

The Pret à Manger chain of takeaways offer some of the highest standards achievable in this type of eatery. The sandwiches are all freshly made on the premises using only the finest ingredients. This philosophy works throughout the chain – wherever you see the name you can be sure of quality.

GLASGOW

Rococo
202 West George Street, Glasgow
Tel 0141 221 5004

Another very fine Glasgow Restaurant, Rococo is run by the same people who have the Bouzy Rouge restaurants. Rococo offers a more formal, fine dining, experience in a contemporary setting. Highly-skilled cooking and excellent service.

GLASGOW

Rogano
11 Exchange Place, Glasgow
Tel 0141 248 4055

Rogano is a Glasgow institution and seems to retain this position regardless of the owners. With its private booths and more formal dining area, it offers either an informal or formal experience to suit needs. Cooking is good yet relatively simple – seafood a speciality. Always a popular meeting place and very much one in which to be seen.

GLASGOW

The Sisters Restaurant
29 Ashton Lane
Glasgow G12 8SJ
Tel 0141 337 3636
Fax 01355 222044
Web www.sistersrestaurant.com

Located in trendy Ashton Lane this is a

small and intimate restaurant which specialises in simply, yet skilfully, cooked dishes made from only the best local produce. A not so well-kept secret which meets expectations.

GLASGOW

Stravaigin
28 Gibson Street, Hillhead
Glasgow G12 8NX
Tel 0141 334 2665
Fax 0141 334 4099
email bookings@stravaigin.com
Web www.stravaigin.com

Stravaigin was the first Glasgow restaurant opened by Colin Clydesdale. It is a stylish and popular venue where the food is king. The produce is superb and the cooking highly skilled, justifiably recognised and consistently good.

GLASGOW

Stravaigin 2
8 Ruthven Lane
Glasgow G12 9BG
Tel 0141 334 7165
Fax 0141 357 4785
email mailbox@stravaigin2.com
Web www.stravaigin.com

Stravaigin 2 is the sister restaurant to Stravaigin, also run by Colin Clydesdale. The cooking – contemporary Scottish with fusion influences – is excellent. An informal and welcoming establishment.

GLASGOW

Ubiquitous Chip
12 Ashton Lane
Glasgow G12 8SJ

Tel 0141 334 5007
Fax 0141 337 1302
email mail@ubiquitouschip.co.uk
Web www.ubiquitouschip.co.uk

One of Glasgow's finest eateries the 'Chip' is run by Ronnie Clydesdale who has been advocating the use of the very best Scottish produce for over 34 years and has been recognised many times over for his imaginative and skillful approach. Scottish Game Cookery Award 2003

GLENCOE

The Coffee Shop
Crafts & Things
Glencoe
Argyll
PA49 4HN
Tel 01855 811325
email david@glencoe.u-net.com
Web www.glencoe.u-net.com

Crafts and Things is located on the A82 near the Glencoe Crossroads. This attractive coffee shop offers an excellent range of home baking and daily specials – all freshly cooked on site. Well worth visiting.

GLENCOE

The Holly Tree Hotel
Kentallen Pier
Nr Glencoe
Argyll PA38 4BY
Tel 01631 740292
Fax 01631 740345
email stay@hollytreehotel.co.uk
Web www.hollytreehotel.co.uk

The Holly Tree sits in a delightful location with superb views over Loch Linnhe. The quality of the experience here is definitely superior, ranging from the standard of accommodation, service and the food. Menus here highlight the excellent local produce complemented with home grown salads and herbs. Justifiably popular and memorable.

GLENFINNAN

Glenfinnan Monument
Information Centre, Glenfinnan
Inverness-shire PH37 4LT
Tel 01397 722250
Fax 01397 722250
Web www.nts.org.uk

The Glenfinnan Monument is steeped in history and is another National Trust Property which should be high on the list of anyone interested in Scotland's heritage. The tearoom is at the heart of the centre and offers a tempting range of home baking and light snacks with a stunning outlook.

GLENLIVET

Minmore House Hotel
Glenlivet
Banffshire AB37 9DB
Tel 01807 590378
Fax 01807 590472
email minmorehouse@ukonline.co.uk
Web www.minmorehousehotel.com

Minmore is a wonderful small hotel which is both comfortable and congenial. The hosts are unobtrusively professional and really make guests feel at home. The cooking is quite superb, skilful and innovative and using the highest quality local produce. A very special place.

GLENLUCE

Kelvin House Hotel
53 Main Street, Glenluce
Wigtownshire DG8 0PP
Tel 01581 300303
Fax 01581 300303
email kelvinhouse@lineone.net
Web www.kelvin-house.co.uk

Kelvin House Hotel is a small, friendly hotel which is ideally located for exploring Galloway. The restaurant offers an enticing range of traditionally prepared local produce served by friendly staff in comfortable surroundings.

GLENROTHES

The Orangery
Balbirnie House Hotel
Balbirnie Park
Markinch
Glenrothes
Fife KY7 6NE
Tel 01592 610066
Fax 01592 610529
email info@balbirnie.co.uk
Web www.balbirnie.co.uk

Balbirnie is widely recognised as one of Scotland's top privately-owned hotels. Owned and run by the Russell family, this hotel has been recognised for consistently achieving the highest of standards in both accommodation and cooking. The food here is of an exemplary standard, featuring skilfully prepared and presented local produce, served in elegant surroundings by attentive staff. 4 AA Red Stars. RAC Gold Ribbon

GLENSHIEL

Duich House
Letterfearn
Glenshiel
Ross-shire
IV40 8HS
Tel 01599 555259
Fax 01599 555259/555333
email ail@duichhouse.co.uk
Web www.duichhouse.co.uk

Duich House is a small, very comfortable house where owners Bill and Anne are welcoming hosts. The cooking here reflects the owners' experience in the Far East. Bill is a skilled cook and makes best use of local produce.

GRANTOWN-ON-SPEY

Auchendean Lodge Hotel
Dulnain Bridge, Grantown-on-Spey
Inverness-shire PH26 3LU
Tel 01479 851347
Fax 01479 851347
email hotel@auchendean.com
Web www.auchendean.com

Auchendean is a real gem, run by
Eric and Ian, convivial and
accomplished hosts who make you
feel most welcome. The house is
particularly charming and
comfortable and the menus and
cooking are a testament to the
passion and interest in quality
produce and exquisite flavours.

GRANTOWN-ON-SPEY

Brooklynn
Grant Road
Grantown-on-Spey
PH26 3LA
Tel 01479 873113
email brooklynn@woodier.com
Web www.woodier.com

Brooklyn is a high-quality guest house
where hosts are very welcoming.
Menus are well balanced and take
account of guests' preferences. Cooking
is of a very high standard: good local
produce used with care and some
modern influences.

GRANTOWN-ON-SPEY

Culdearn House Hotel
Woodlands Terrace, Grantown-on-Spey
Morayshire PH26 3JU
Tel 01479 872106
Fax 01479 873641
email culdearn@globalnet.co.uk
Web www.culdearn.com

Culdearn may now be under new
ownership, but it remains a supremely
comfortable guest house offering a
high standard of welcome and all-
round experience to guests.

GRANTOWN-ON-SPEY

Muckrach Lodge
Finlarig, Dulnain Bridge
Grantown on Spey
Inverness-shire PH26 3LY
Tel 01479 851257
Fax 01479 851325

Muckrach Lodge is an excellent small
hotel where the owners take great
pride in achieving the standards they
aspire to. The hotel is very comfortable
and staff are attentive and friendly.
Cooking is highly accomplished, only
using the best quality, locally-sourced
produce.

GRANTOWN-ON-SPEY

The Pines
Woodside Avenue
Grantown-on-Spey PH26 3JR
Tel 01479 872092
Fax 01479 872092
email info@thepinesgrantown.co.uk
Web www.thepinesgrantown.co.uk

The Pines, run by Michael and Gwen
Stewart, is a very comfortable and in
many ways unique house. Michael is a
most welcoming host and Gwen's
cooking is particularly outstanding,
using excellent local produce, cooked
with real care and attention to detail.

GULLANE

Golf Inn
Main Street
Gullane
EH31 2AB
Tel 01620 842655

The Golf Inn has long been a popular venue to enjoy really good bar meals. It is popular with golfers, locals and visitors and offers a warm welcome and fine food in relaxing surroundings.

GULLANE

Greywalls
Muirfield
Gullane
East Lothian
EH31 2EG
Tel 01620 842144
Fax 01620 842241
email hotel@greywalls.co.uk
Web www.greywalls.co.uk

Greywalls is a famous historic hotel discreetly located within a beautiful walled garden. The hotel is elegant, comfortable and extremely well run. The cooking here is excellent, skilfully prepared and presented by a talented team who use only the best ingredients.

GULLANE

La Potiniere
Gullane
East Lothian
Tel 01620 843214

La Potiniere was long recognised as one of the best eating places in Scotland, if not a little quirky. Now, however, after a short gap, it has been taken over by Keith and Mary who have quickly established their own particular style and standards. An ideal place to enjoy good food in convivial surroundings.

HADDINGTON

Maitlandfield House Hotel
24 Sidegate, Haddington
East Lothian EH41 4BZ
Tel 01620 826513
Fax 01620 826713
email ndf@maitlandfieldhouse.co.uk
Web www.maitlandfieldhouse.co.uk

Maitlandfield House is a comfortable hotel, which has been gradually upgraded under its present owners. It offers a variety of locations to eat to suit all occasions, and the standard of cooking is good with an interesting Portuguese influence.

HADDINGTON

The Waterside
Haddington
East Lothian
Tel 01620 825674

The Waterside is a well-established favourite and, whilst it's now owned by a major brewery, the standard is still very high. There is a bar/bistro downstairs and more formal dining upstairs.

HARRIS, ISLE OF

Leachin House
Tarbert, Isle of Harris
Outer Hebrides HS3 3AH
Tel 01859 502157
Fax 01859 502157
email leachin.house@virgin.net
Web www.leachin-house.com

Leachin House is a delightful place to stay and enjoy this magical corner of the Hebrides. The hosts have built up a justifiable reputation for their hospitality and very high standard of cooking. Interesting menus naturally focus on some of the great Hebridean produce on the doorstep. Western Isles Tourist Board – 4 Star Guest House, 3 Medallion Home Cooking

HARRIS, ISLE OF

Scarista House
Isle of Harris HS3 3HX
Tel 01859 550238
Fax 01859 550277
email timandpatricia@scaristahouse.com
Web www.scaristahouse.com

Scarista has long been recognised as a particularly attractive place to enjoy the unique experience in the Hebrides. Tim and Patricia Martin are accomplished and welcoming hosts and offer the highest standard from accommodation to the wonderful meals using local produce and home grown herbs. Good for the Soul Award – Scottish Hotels of the Year.

HAWICK

Mansfield House Hotel
Weensland Road
Hawick TD9 8LB
Tel 01450 360400
Fax 01450 372007

email ian@mansfield-house.com
Web www.mansfield-house.com

A family-owned and run hotel, The Mansfield is popular with locals and visitors. It is comfortable and the welcome is genuine and friendly. The standard of cooking is impressive, with particular emphasis on choice Borders produce.

HELENSBURGH

Hill House
Upper Colquhoun Street
Helensburgh
G84 9AJ
Tel 01436 673900
Fax 01436 674685
Web www.nts.org.uk

Hill House is another exciting National Trust for Scotland property – a 'must visit' for lovers of Charles Rennie Mackintosh. There is a fine coffee shop where you can enjoy the splendid surroundings with a good choice of home baking and light snacks.

HOWWOOD

The Country Club Restaurant
Bowfield Hotel & Country Club
Howwood
Renfrewshire
PA9 1DB
Tel 01505 705225
Fax 01505 705230
email enquiries@
bowfieldcountryclub.co.uk
Web www.bowfieldcountryclub.co.uk

Bowfield Hotel and Country Club is a country retreat with a full complement of leisure facilities. It is popular with international and local visitors and offers a relaxed dining experience. The cooking here is imaginative and of good quality and the service is friendly and informal.

INNERLEITHEN

Caddon View
14 Pirn Road
Innerleithen
EH44 6HH
Tel 01896 830208
Web www.caddonview.co.uk

Caddon View is a small, charming and very comfortable hotel. Here you will find a blend of informal hospitality combined with marvellous cooking which has a French influence.

INNERLEITHEN

Traquair Arms Hotel
Traquair Road
Innerleithen
Peebles-shire
EH44 6PD
Tel 01896 830229
Fax 01896 830260
email traquair.arms@scottishborders.com
Web www.traquair-arms-hotel.co.uk

Traquair Arms is a small country hotel near to Traquair House with its famous brewery. The cooking is good and hearty and uses fresh local ingredients.

INVERKEILOR

Gordon's Restaurant with Rooms
Main Street
Inverkeilor
By Arbroath
DD1 5RN
Tel 01241 830364
Fax 01241 830364
email gordonsrest@aol.com
Web www.gordonsrestaurant.co.uk

Gordon's Restaurant, run by Gordon, Maria and Garry Watson, is another of Scotland's finest. Everything possible is made on the premises and the cooking skills are second to none. A very special place indeed. 2 AA Rosettes, Master Chef of Great Britain, STB 4 Stars

INVERNESS

Bunchrew House Hotel
Bunchrew
Inverness IV3 8TA
Tel 01463 234917
Fax 01463 710620
email welcome@
bunchrewinverness.co.uk
Web www.bunchrew-inverness.co.uk

Bunchrew is an imposing country mansion located on the outskirts of Inverness. This is a very comfortable hotel with an elegant dining room where menus offer a good selection of Scottish produce, expertly prepared and presented by a talented team.

INVERNESS

Café 1
75 Castle Street
Inverness IV2 3EA
Tel 01463 226200
Fax 01463 716363
email info@cafe1.net
Web www.cafe1.net

Small, friendly and informal, Café 1 is centrally located in the city of Inverness. It is an excellent restaurant where Scottish cooking or real quality is prepared and presented in an innovative style.

INVERNESS

Culloden Moor Visitor Centre Restaurant
Culloden Moor
Inverness IV2 5EU
Tel 01463 790607
Fax 01463 794294
email macintosh@nts.org.uk
Web www.nts.org.uk

No visit to this area would be complete without a visit to the atmospheric Culloden Moor. The tearoom here – run by the National Trust – offers an extensive range of home-made soups, home baking and light snacks.

INVERNESS

Drumossie Park Cottage
Inverness
IV2 5BB
Tel 01463 224127
Fax 01463 224127
email j.naismith@talk21.com
Web www.scotland-info.co.uk/drumossie

Drumossie is a small, welcoming Bed and Breakfast which is run by a very welcoming and attentive hostess. The cooking is of an excellent standard using quality local produce.

INVERNESS

Dunain Park Hotel
Inverness
IV3 8JN
Tel 01463 230512
Fax 01463 224532
email dunainparkhotel@btinternet.com
Web www.dunainparkhotel.co.uk

Dunain Park, on the outskirts of Inverness, is a very comfortable hotel with excellent amenities and accommodation in beautiful surroundings. The cooking here is exceptional – highly accomplished and using good local produce, prepared and presented with skill.

INVERNESS

The Glenmhor Hotel
9-12 Ness Bank
Inverness IV2 4SG
Tel 01463 234308
Fax 01463 713170
email glenmhor@ukonline.co.uk
Web www.glen-mohr.com

Sitting on the banks of the River Ness, Glenmhor Hotel is home to one of the best hotel restaurants in the area. Nico's speciality is seafood which is produced with continental influences, although the meat dishes, prepared and presented with imagination and skill, are equally good.

INVERNESS

The Lodge at Daviot Mains
Daviot, Inverness
Inverness-shire IV2 5ER
Tel 01463 772215
Fax 01463 772099
email info@thelodge-daviotmains.co.uk
Web www.thelodge-daviotmains.co.uk

Alex and Margaret Hutcheson are accomplished hosts who now operate from their recently-built home which is spacious, comfortable and built in a traditional Highland style. The cooking here is accomplished, making best use of good local produce, prepared with skill and balance. STB 4 Stars

INVERNESS

The Maple Court Hotel
12 Ness Walk
Inverness IV3 5SQ
Tel 01463 230330
Fax 01463 237700
email maplecourt@macleodhotels.co.uk
Web www.macleodhotels.co.uk

Maple Court is in a quiet location on the outskirts of the city. The cooking here is of a high standard and is modern Scottish in style, making imaginative use of locally-sourced game and seafood.

INVERNESS

Restaurant Chez Christophe
16 Ardross St
Inverness IV3 5NS
Tel 01463 717126
Fax 01463 717126
email info@chezchristophe.co.uk
Web www.chezchristophe.co.uk

Chez Christophe is a stunningly good French restaurant. It is small and comfortable and the commitment to the highest of standards evident throughout. This is a special place to enjoy the finest Scottish produce prepared with classic French style and skill.

INVERNESS

Royal Highland Hotel
Station Square
Inverness
IV1 1LG
Tel 01463 231926
Fax 01463 710705
email info@royalhighlandhotel.co.uk
Web www.royalhighlandhotel.com

This centrally-located hotel offers a high
standard of accommodation and food.
The cooking here is of a traditional
Scottish style with creative touches.

INVERNESS

**Seafields Restaurant at
The Taste of Moray**
Gollanfield
Inverness IV2 7QT
Tel 01667 462340
Fax 01667 461087
email neil@scottishgourmetfood.co.uk
Web www.scottishgourmetfood.co.uk

Seafields Restaurant and Grill is a
combination of food and cookshop with
a fine restaurant in there for good
measure. The food here is substantial
and varied and offers everything from
tea and coffee and home baking to
light snacks served by friendly staff.

INVERURIE

Simpson's Restaurant
**Macdonald Thainstone House
Hotel**
Inverurie
Aberdeenshire
AB51 5NT
Tel 01467 621643
Fax 01467 625084
email reservations@
thainstone.macdonald-hotels.co.uk
Web www.macdonaldhotels.co.uk

Located on the outskirts of Inverurie,
Thainstone House Hotel is a charming,
well-maintained and renovated house.
This grand mansion offers superlative
accommodation, service and food in
Simpson's Restaurant, where skill and
quality are much in evidence.

ISLAY, ISLE OF

The Croft Kitchen
Port Charlotte
Isle of Islay
PA48 7UD
Tel 01496 850 230
Fax 01496 850 230
email douglas@
croftkitchen.demon.co.uk

The Croft Kitchen is an unassuming
establishment but one which is very
popular with locals and visitors. Here
you can enjoy a superb range of fresh
produce, home bakes, snacks and daily
specials simply but attractively
prepared and presented.

ISLAY, ISLE OF

Glenmachrie Country Guest House
Port Ellen
Isle of Islay
PA42 7AW
Tel 01496 302560
Fax 01496 302560
email glenmachrie@lineone.net
Web www.glenmachrie.com

This family-run working farmhouse has
been exceptionally well-run by Rachel
Whyte for many years and to great
acclaim. Guests' comfort is her first
priority and in this she clearly succeeds.
The cooking here is also of a very high
standard, making best use of locally-
sourced produce, expertly prepared and
presented.

ISLAY, ISLE OF

The Harbour Inn
The Square
Bowmore
Isle of Islay
PA43 7JR
Tel 01496 810330
Fax 01496 810990
email harbour@harbour-inn.com
Web www.harbour-inn.com

As its name suggests, the Harbour Inn sits by the harbour in Bowmore and has superb views over the bay. This is a delightful family-run Inn which has been rightly recognised for the quality and commitment to fresh local produce. Chef Proprietor Scott Chance is highly proficient and produces dishes which are well balanced and tastefully presented.

ISLAY, ISLE OF

Kilmeny Country Guest House
Ballygrant
Isle of Islay
PA45 7QW
Tel 01496 840668
Fax 01496 840668
email info@kilmeny.co.uk
Web www.kilmeny.co.uk

Kilmeny Country House is a delight, run by Margaret Rozga who takes a great deal of care and effort to ensure guests are made comfortable. The house is charming and rooms are tastefully furnished. Cooking here is excellent, too, everything being home-made and locally sourced. This is a very special dining experience where you can really enjoy skilled Scottish cooking in beautiful surroundings.

JEDBURGH

Caddy Man
Mounthooley
Jedburgh TD8 6TJ
Tel 01835 850787
Fax 01835 850787

The Caddy Man is a charming, warm and welcoming restaurant where the menus are interesting and feature local produce. The cooking is skilled and the service is friendly. Everything is freshly prepared on the premises – look out for the superb home bakes! Winner Best Promotion Local Produce 2002

JEDBURGH

Restaurant Bardoulet
Jedforest Hotel
Nr Jedburgh
Roxburghshire TD8 6PJ
Tel 01835 840222
Fax 01835 840226
email mail@jedforesthotel.freeserve.co.uk
Web www.jedforesthotel.freeserve.co.uk

Jedforest Hotel is proud to be the first hotel you reach as you enter Scotland from over the border. It is a very high standard of small hotel, comfortably furnished and the staff are welcoming and friendly. The cooking here is excellent, making good use of best Borders produce and prepared with flair and skill.

KELSO

Ednam House Hotel
Bridge Street
Kelso TD5 7HT
Tel 01573 224168
Fax 01573 226319
email contact@ednamhouse.com
Web www.ednamhouse.com

Ednam House Hotel is a comfortable and friendly hotel where the service is attentive. The cooking is of a very high standard offering good local produce which is cooked with international influences and flair.

KELSO

Queens Bistro
24 Bridge Street
Kelso
Tel 01573 228899
Fax 01573 228899

Gary Moore is a highly talented Chef whose reputation goes before him. Here you can enjoy the very best of local produce prepared and presented by a highly skilled Chef in warm and convivial surroundings.

KELSO

The Roxburghe Hotel & Golf Course
Heiton
By Kelso
TD5 8JZ
Tel 01573 450331
Fax 01573 450611
email hotel@roxburghe.net
Web www.roxburghe.net

The Roxburghe Hotel and Golf Course is set in a beautiful estate and is a superb country house, luxuriously appointed. The cooking here is highly skilled by an accomplished chef who makes best use of the finest Borders produce.

KELTY

Kathellan
Cocklaw Mains Farm
Kelty
Fife
KY4 OJR
Tel 01383 830169
Fax 01383 831614
email enquiries@butterchurn.co.uk
Web www.butterchurn.co.uk

Now under new ownership, this remains an excellent place to enjoy a browse in the well-stocked shop and then enjoy some excellent home cooking, home baking and light meals.

KILLEARN

Conservatory Restaurant
The Black Bull
2 The Square
Killearn
G63 9NG
Tel 01360 550215
Fax 01360 550143
email info@theblackbull-killearn.co.uk

This hotel, in the centre of Killearn, is an excellent place to enjoy the very best of modern Scottish cooking. The Conservatory Restaurant is stylish and contemporary and the menus reflect this style using fresh local produce prepared and presented in a modern and sympathetic manner.

KILLIN

Dalerb
Craignavie Road
Killin
FK21 8SH
Tel 01567 820961
Fax 01567 820043
email k.fitzgerald@virgin.net
Web www.dalerb.com

This is a relatively new Bed and Breakfast which has quickly established itself a comfortable and welcoming destination. Hosts are accomplished and ensure that guests enjoy peace and tranquillity during their stay. The cooking is of a very high standard and uses only locally-sourced produce.

THE
BLACK BULL
HOTEL

*D*INING AT THE BLACK BULL HOTEL IS A CIVILISED
ADULT AFFAIR... LOW LIGHTING, CRISP LINEN, STYLISH
SURROUNDINGS AND DELICIOUS FOOD

*U*LTIMATELY THE BLACK BULL HOTEL IS ALL
ABOUT... CUSTOMER SERVICE

2 The Square, Killearn, Stirlingshire G63 9NG
Telephone: +44 (0)1360 550215
Fax: +44 (0)1360 550143
Email: sales@blackbullhotel.com
www.blackbullhotel.com

KILLIN

Fairview House
Main Street
Killin
FK21 8UT
Tel 01567 820667
email info@fairview-killin.co.uk
Web www.fairview-killin.co.uk

Fairview House is a very well appointed guest house which is located in the centre of the village. The hosts are welcoming, the atmosphere relaxing and the meals here reflect high standards of home cooking.

KILWINNING

Montgreenan Mansion House Hotel
Montgreenan Estate
nr Kilwinning
Ayrshire
KA13 7QZ
Tel 01294 557733
Fax 01294 850397
email info@montgreenanhotel.com
Web www.montgreenanhotel.com

Montgreenan Mansion is an elegant country house hotel which has been extensively and attractively refurbished. Service is accomplished and in keeping with the style of the property, and the dining is a very high standard of modern Scottish in fine surroundings.

KILMARNOCK

The Fenwick Hotel
A77 Ayr Road
Kilmarnock
Ayrshire KA3 6AU
Tel 01560 600478
Fax 01560 600334
email fenwick@bestwestern.co.uk
Web www.fenwickhotel.co.uk

This busy hotel is ideally located on the A77 at Fenwick and is a popular meeting place. The bistro is comfortably furnished and the cooking is modern Scottish with an emphasis on local produce, skilfully prepared and presented.

KILMARNOCK

Nether Underwood
By Symington
Kilmarnock
Ayrshire KA1 5NG
Tel 01563 830666
Fax 01563 830777
email netherund@aol.com
Web www.netherunderwood.co.uk

Nether Underwood is a small but elegant and well-appointed Guest House. Hostess Felicity Thomson is accomplished and takes care to look after guests well. Currently dinner is not available but this lovely place is still worthy of mention as the standard of breakfast offered is so very high!

KILMARTIN

Kilmartin House Museum Café
Kilmartin
Argyll PA31 8RQ
Tel 01546 510278
Fax 01546 510330
email museum@kilmartin.org
Web www.kilmartin.org

Kilmartin House Museum Café is an ideal place to stop and take in some of the best of local produce. The tearoom offers an extensive range of light lunches and home bakes which are available all day.

KINBUCK

The Restaurant at Cromlix
Cromlix House
Kinbuck
Nr Dunblane
Perthshire FK15 9JT
Tel 01786 822125
Fax 01786 825450
email reservations@cromlixhouse.com
Web www.cromlixhouse.com

Cromlix is one of the most appealing country houses in Scotland. The house even has its own charming chapel. This elegant property is a comfortable relaxing place to enjoy the good life and superb service. The menus are classic Scottish with a modern twist and the cooking is highly skilled!

KINCARDINE-ON-FORTH

The Unicorn Inn
15 Excise Street
Kincardine-on-Forth
Fife FK10 4LN
email Budde@unicorninn.fs.net.co.uk

The Unicorn Inn has been recently refurbished to a very high standard. Still expertly run by Liz and Tony Budde, this contemporary bistro offers the very best of Scottish produce skilfully cooked. Menus offer something so suit every taste – this is well worth a visit.

KINCRAIG

March House
Feshiebridge
Kincraig
Inverness-shire
PH21 1NG
Tel 01540 651388
Fax 01540 651388
email caroline@kincraig.com
Web www.kincraig.com/march

In an ideal location, March House is a superb Guest House where the hostess really knows how to make guests feel at home. The house itself is very comfortable and the menus are modern, using all fresh local produce which is carefully prepared and presented. STB 3 Star Guest House

KINGUSSIE

Columba House Hotel & Garden Restaurant
Manse Road
Kingussie
Inverness-shire
PH21 1JF
Tel 01540 661402
Fax 01540 661652
email reservations@columbahousehotel.com
Web www.columbahousehotel.com

Columba House Hotel is a small hotel which is exceptional in terms of both hospitality and surroundings. It is in an ideal location for lovers of the outdoors and offers a high standard of service and cooking to guests.

KINGUSSIE

The Cross

Tweed Mill Brae
Ardbroilach Road, Kingussie
Inverness-shire PH21 1TC
Tel 01540 661166
Fax 01540 661080
email fabulousfood@thecross.co.uk
Web www.thecross.co.uk

The Cross is in an idyllic position in a converted tweed mill. A superb small hotel and excellent restaurant, it offers a rather special dining experience with service to match.

KINGUSSIE

The Osprey Hotel

Ruthven Road, Kingussie
Inverness-shire PH21 1EN
Tel 01540 661510
Fax 01540 661510
email aileen@ospreyhotel.co.uk
Web www.ospreyhotel.co.uk

The Osprey Hotel is a welcoming small hotel. The hosts are accomplished and the cooking is of a very high standard, using only top quality local produce. AA 5 Diamond.

KINLOCH RANNOCH

Bunrannoch House

Kinloch Rannoch
Perthshire PH16 5QB
Tel 01882 632407
Fax 01882 632407
email bun.house@tesco.net
Web www.bunrannoch.co.uk

Jennifer Skeaping is a welcoming Chef

Proprietor. Bunrannoch is a comfortable, friendly house. Menus are interesting, well thought out and all food is freshly sourced and cooked with skill and care.

KINLOCH RANNOCH

Dunalastair Hotel

The Square, Kinloch Rannoch
Perthshire PH16 5PW
Tel 01882 632218
Fax 01882 632371
email reserve@dunalastair.co.uk
Web www.dunalastair.co.uk

Dunalastair Hotel is an impressive country hotel which has been carefully restored. Accommodation is very comfortable and the food served is good local produce which is prepared with great attention to detail and some modern touches.

KINROSS

Carlin Maggies

191 High Street, Kinross
Tayside KY13 8DB
Tel 01577 863652
Fax 01577 863652

Carlin Maggies is set right in the heart of Kinross and is a comfortable and welcoming restaurant. The food here has an international feel to it whilst still using locally sourced ingredients. Look out for the excellent daily specials.

KIRKBEAN

Cavens

Kirkbean
Dumfriesshire DG2 8AA
Tel 01387 880234
Fax 01387 880467

email enquiries@cavens.com
Web www.cavens.com

Cavens is a real gem. Angus and Jane run this comfortable country house with flair and style. The cooking is superb, combining skilfull and modern use of fresh local produce, all beautifully presented.

KIRKCALDY

The Oswald Room
Dunnikier House Hotel
Dunnikier Park
Kirkcaldy KY1 3LP
Tel 01592 268393
Fax 01592 642340
email recp@dunnikier-house-hotel.co.uk
Web www.dunnikier-house-hotel.co.uk

Dunnikier House Hotel is run be Barry and Kay Bridgens and has superb views over the Firth of Forth. It is particularly popular for business lunches and offers a very high standard of Scottish cuisine with French influences.

KIRKCUDBRIGHT

The Selkirk Arms Hotel
High Street, Kirkcudbright
Dumfries & Galloway DG6 4JG
Tel 01557 330402
Fax 01557 331639
email reception@selkirkarmshotel.co.uk
Web www.selkirkarmshotel.co.uk

The Selkirk Arms has been trading for over 200 years and has a well deserved reputation for excellent standards of accommodation and service. Menus all feature local produce and specialise in local fish and Galloway beef. Cooking is skilful and the standards are high.

KIRRIEMUIR

**Lochside Lodge &
Roundhouse Restaurant**
Bridgend of Lintrathen
By Kirriemuir DD8 5JJ
Tel 01575 560340

Fax 01575 560202
email enquiries@lochsidelodge.com
Web www.lochsidelodge.com

Lochside Lodge, run by Gail and Graham Riley, is a converted farm steading set in a beautiful location. Menus here are well-balanced and the cooking is highly adept, with imaginative use of local produce. 2 AA Rosesttes. 3 RAC Awards. STB 4 Star Restaurant with Rooms. Shortlisted Flavour of Scotland Awards – 2004.

KYLE

The Old Schoolhouse
Erbusaig
Kyle
Ross-shire
IV40 8BB
Tel 01599 534369
email cuminecandj@lineone.net
Web www.highland.plus.com/schoolhouse

The Old Schoolhouse is a carefully converted building which now offers a high standard of accommodation to its visitors. The hosts are experienced and welcoming and the food served here is prepared with great skill and imaginative use of fresh local produce.

KYLESKU

Newton Lodge
Kylesku
Sutherland
IV27 4HW
Tel 01971 502070
email newtonlge@aol.com
Web www.smoothhound.co.uk/
hotels/newtonlo.html

Newton Lodge is a small, quiet and comfortable house in peaceful surroundings. Ideal if you're looking for a little tranquillity. The food here is good home cooking which uses local produce and changes daily – meals served at 7pm for residents only.

LAIDE

The Old Smiddy Guest House
Laide
Ross-shire IV22 2NB
Tel 01445 731425
Fax 01445 731696
email oldsmiddy@aol.com
Web www.oldsmiddy.co.uk

Kate Macdonald is a most welcoming
hostess who has thought of every last
detail to ensure her guests' comfort.
The house, too, is warm and
welcoming, and well appointed. Kate's
cooking is simply beautiful – she
makes the best use of local produce
and brings experience and imagination
to all of her dishes.

LANGHOLM

The Reivers Rest
High Street, Langholm
Dumfriesshire DG13 0DJ
Tel 013873 81343
Fax 013873 81343
email mail@reivers-rest.co.uk
Web www.reivers-rest.co.uk

This 240-year-old Inn is a warm and
friendly place to enjoy good food in
convivial surroundings. The lounge bar
is cosy and the menus are interesting
and use only good local produce.
Cooking is of a high standard with
some innovative twists.

LAUDER

The Lodge at Carfraemill
Lauder
Berwickshire TD2 6RA
Tel 01578 750750

Fax 01578 750751
email enquiries@carfraemill.co.uk
Web www.carfraemill.co.uk

Carfraemill is a great meeting place –
located at the crossroads on the A68 it
is impossible to miss. Whether for a
coffee stop or lunch or dinner, this is
popular with locals and visitors. The
cooking is of an excellent standard –
locally sourced and menus are
traditional. Good for all the family.
STB 3 Medallions. Winner – Best Tastes
Competition, Borders Tourist Board,
2003.

LAURENCEKIRK

Tower Restaurant
Laurencekirk Business Park
Aberdeen Road
Laurencekirk
AB30 1EY
Tel 01561 378123
Fax 01561 378379
email stewart@towerres1.fsnet.co.uk

The Tower is an excellent fish and chip
shop in the Laurencekirk Business Park
with ample parking. It serves a wide
range of dishes, all freshly prepared to
order and there is a special children's
menu.

LESLIE

Rescobie House Hotel
6 Valley Drive
Leslie
KY6 3BQ
Tel 01592 749555
Fax 01592 620231
Web www.rescobie-hotel.co.uk

Rescobie House Hotel incorporates a
most attractive restaurant in charming
listed surroundings. Menus from the
talented Chef include good locally-
sourced produce which is prepared and
presented with flair.

LEWIS, ISLE OF

Bonaventure
Aird Uig
Timsgarry
Isle of Lewis
HS2 9JA
Tel 01851 672474

This is a small island restaurant which has been much acclaimed by those who have been fortunate enough to experience it. The cooking is skilled and uses good local produce which is cooked with French influence. This is an unusual but superior restaurant and well worth seeking out when in the area.

LEWIS, ISLE OF

Digby Chick Restaurant
11 James Street
Stornoway
Isle of Lewis
HS1 2QN
Tel 01851 706600
Fax 01851 703900

Digby Chick is a small, unpretentious restaurant dedicated to serving a delicious selection of local dishes and many more traditional favourites. A friendly restaurant offering a range of meals to suit all tastes.

LEWIS, ISLE OF

Park Guest House & Restaurant
30 James Street, Stornoway
Isle of Lewis HS1 2QN
Tel 01851 702485
Fax 01851 703482

Centrally located in Stornoway, Park Guest House is an excellent place to base yourself. Roddy and Catherine Afrin are welcoming and thoughtful hosts who take great pride in the quality and range that they offer. Dishes are skilfully prepared, thoughtfully composed and well presented to make the best use of local produce.

LINLITHGOW

Champany Inn
Linlithgow
West Lothian
Tel 01506 834532

Champany's is a mecca for lovers of the best quality beef. This restaurant has two dining options – one less formal than the other. The menus are traditional – the cooking is skilled and the ambience welcoming. A charming inn where the quality is indisputable.

LINLITHGOW

Livingston's Restaurant
52 High Street
Linlithgow
EH49 7AE
Tel 01506 846565
Fax 01506 846565

Livingston's Restaurant is a superb restaurant tucked away behind the High Street in the shadow of Linlithgow Palace. The cooking here is of a consistently high standard and the ambience is relaxed and welcoming. Menus are modern Scottish in style and use only quality local produce which is presented with skill.

LINLITHGOW

Marynka
57 High Street
Linlithgow
West Lothian
EH49 7ED
Tel 01506 840123
Fax 01506 843130
email eat@marynka.com
Web www.marynka.com

Marynka is a friendly stylish restaurant centrally located in the High Street. It offers interesting menus and highly accomplished cooking which is beautifully presented.

LOCH MAREE

The Old Mill Highland Lodge
Talladale, Loch Maree
Ross-shire IV22 2HL
Tel 01445 760271
email Jo.Powell@bosinternet.com
Web www.theoldmillhighlandlodge.co.uk

This excellent small hotel is run by efficient and welcoming hosts. The lodge is very comfortable and the standard of cooking and presentation high. Here you will enjoy a unique and pleasurable experience.

LOCH TORRIDON

Shieldaig Bar
Shieldaig
Loch Torridon
Ross-shire
IV54 8XN
Tel 01520 755251
Fax 01520 755321
email tighaneileanhotel@
shieldaig.fsnet.co.uk

Shieldaig Bar is an excellent bar which is popular with locals and visitors. You'll find a very high standard of bar food which uses fresh local produce and superb home baking to complement the dishes.

LOCH TORRIDON

Tigh an Eilean Hotel
Shieldaig, Loch Torridon
Ross-shire IV54 8XN
Tel 01520 755251
Fax 01520 755321
email tighaneileanhotel@
shieldaig.fsnet.co.uk

Tigh an Eilean is an excellent, really charming small hotel, set in a superb location on the shores of Loch Torridon. The cooking is also first class, inspired use of local produce is enhanced with some French influences. 2 AA Rosettes. AA Top 200 Hotels in the UK 2004/5

LOCHCARRON

Rockvilla Hotel
Main Street
Lochcarron IV54 8YB
Tel 01520 722379
Fax 01520 722844
email richardmunro@rockvilla-hotel.co.uk
Web www.rockvilla-hotel.co.uk

Rockvilla is a small, rural family-run hotel. The restaurant offers menus which mainly use quality local produce prepared in a traditional style to a high standard.

BY LOCHGILPHEAD

Buidhe Lodge
Craobh Haven, By Lochgilphead
Argyll PA31 8UA
Tel 01852 500291
email simone&buidhelodge.com
Web www.buidhelodge.com

Buidhe Lodge is a traditional wooden

lodge. It is a small, very attractive guest house where you will find cooking to be savoured. Everything is home made and uses local produce in the guests' set menu.

BY LOCHGILPHEAD

Cairnbaan Hotel
Cairnbaan, By Lochgilphead
Argyll PA31 8SJ
Tel 01546 603668
Fax 01546 606045
email cairnbaan.hotel@virgin.net
Web www.cairnbaan.com

Cairnbaan is a very fine small hotel which is in a unique location by the picturesque Crinan Canal. The restaurant has an enviable reputation for the quality of its locally-caught seafood, cooked with skill and care in a traditional style.

BY LOCHGILPHEAD

Crinan Hotel
Crinan, Lochgilphead
Argyll PA31 8SR
Tel 01546 830261
Fax 01546 830292
email nryan@crinanhotel.com
Web www.crinanhotel.com

For many years now, Crinan Hotel has been popular base from which to enjoy this beautiful location. The hotel itself is both appealing and welcoming. There is a choice of dining options – in all, however, the standard of freshly prepared local produce, especially seafood, is superb.

LOCHINVER

The Albannach
Lochinver
Sutherland IV27 4LP
Tel 01571 84440
Fax 01571 844285
email the.albannach@virgin.net

The Albannach is quite simply a gem.

Lesley Crosfield and Colin Craig have restored this lovely house into an outstanding small hotel where they offer a unique experience. The standard of cooking here is exquisite and innovative with the emphasis on taste and quality local produce.

LOCHWINNOCH

East Lochhead Country House & Cottages
Largs Road
Lochwinnoch
Renfrewshire
PA12 4DX
Tel 01505 842610
Fax 01505 842610
Web www.eastlochhead.co.uk

East Lochhead has been justifiably recognised for the high level of quality offered by Janet and Ross Anderson. The house is set in a beautiful garden and the standard of comfort is exceptionally high. Janet's cooking is superb and stylish, using only good locally-sourced produce.

LOCKERBIE

Dryfesdale Hotel
Dryfebridge
Lockerbie
Dumfries
DG11 2SF
Tel 01576 202427
Fax 01576 204187
email reception@dryfesdalehotel.co.uk
Web www.dryfesdalehotel.co.uk

Dryfesdale Hotel is a attractive and well-appointed hotel set in an elevated position with fine views of the surrounding countryside. Dining here is invariably a pleasure, with well-balanced menus reflecting the local produce available. Cooking is to a high standard, both skilful and knowledgeable.

LUNDIN LINKS

Aithernie Restaurant
The Old Manor Country House Hotel
Leven Road, Lundin Links
Near St Andrews KY8 6AJ
Tel 01333 320368
Fax 01333 320911
email enquiries@oldmanorhotel.co.uk
Web www.oldmanorhotel.co.uk

The Old Manor Hotel is popular with locals and visitors. Ideally located in the East Neuk village of Lundin Links, it offers high standards throughout. There are a range of dining options here – all offering the best of local produce, adroitly prepared and presented.

LUSS

The Coach House Coffee Shop
Luss, Loch Lomond
Argyll G83 8NN
Tel 01436 860341
Fax 01436 860336
email enquiries@
lochlomondtrading.com
Web www.lochlomondtrading.com

The Coach House Coffee Shop is run by Gary and Rowena Groves who are passionate about the quality of everything they do. This coffee shop is warm and welcoming and the standard of light meals and home baking is superb. An interesting range of Scottish crafts in the shop complete this experience. Macallan Award Winner

LUSS

Lodge on Loch Lomond Hotel & Restaurant
Luss
Argyll G83 8PA
Tel 01460 860201
Fax 01460 860203
email lusslomond@aol.com
Web www.loch-lomond.co.uk

In a beautiful location on the shores of

Loch Lomond, The Lodge is a comfortable and relaxing place to enjoy good food in fine surroundings. Cooking is highly proficient and menus offer a range of dishes to suit all tastes with an emphasis on locally-sourced produce.

LYBSTER

Jo's Kitchen, Library & Bistro Bar
The Portland Arms Hotel
Lybster
Caithness KW3 6BS
Tel 01593 721721
Fax 01593 721722
email info@portlandarms.co.uk
Web www.portlandarms.co.uk

The Portland Arms is an extremely comfortable and welcoming small hotel. There is a range of dining options to suit the occasion – all of which offer the highest levels of service and cooking with well balanced menus relfecting a strong local influence.

MALLAIG

The Fish Market
Station Road
Mallaig PH41 4QS
Tel 01687 462299
Fax 01687 462623

The Fish Market has a superb location right on the pier – you could not be much closer to the catch! A wide range of seafood is served here, simply prepared and presented to allow the freshness be enjoyed at its best.

MAYBOLE

Visitor Centre Restaurant
The Home Farm
Culzean Castle & Country Park
Maybole, Ayrshire KA19 8LE
Tel 01655 884502
Fax 01655 884521
email whudson@nts.org.uk
Web www.nts.org.uk

Culzean Castle is a stunning National

Trust property, rich in history and occupying a spectacular location. The self-service restaurant at the Home Farm serves a wide range of freshly prepared snacks, home baking and light meals in comfortable and welcoming surroundings.

MELROSE

Burts Hotel
Market Square
Melrose
Scottish Borders TD6 9PL
Tel 01896 822285
Fax 01896 822870
email burtshotel@aol.com
Web www.burtshotel.co.uk

Burts Hotel, run by the Henderson family for many years, has become something of an institution in the Borders. It offers an exceptional standard of welcome both in the bar and in the restaurant. Cooking here is not only skilled but consistently makes best use of local produce. 2 AA Rosettes

MELROSE

Clint Lodge
St Boswells
Melrose TD6 0DZ
Tel 01835 822027
Fax 01835 822656
email clintlodge@aol.com
Web www.clintlodge.co.uk

Clint Lodge is a traditional country house guest house which is comfortable and run by hospitable hosts. Cooking here is to a very high standard, good local produce prepared and presented with taste and style.

MELROSE

Hoebridge Inn Restaurant
Gattonside, Melrose TD6 9LZ
Tel 01896 823082

The Hoebridge Inn is a charming and relaxing place to enjoy good local produce, which is skillfully prepared and attractively presented.

MELROSE

The Old School
Bowden, nr Melrose
Roxburghshire TD6 0SS
Tel 01835 822228
Web www.theoldschooltearoom.co.uk

The Old School tearoom is a traditional relaxing place to indulge in the most enjoyable cooking and home baking which makes extremely good use of locally-sourced produce. A great place to experience traditional Borders hospitality.

MELROSE

The Townhouse Hotel
Market Square, Melrose TD6 9PQ
Tel 01896 822645
Fax 01896 823474
email Reservations@
thetownhousemelrose.co.uk
Web www.thetownhousemelrose.co.uk

Recently taken over by the Henderson family, The Townhouse Hotel has a stylish new brasserie which has been tastefully refurbished by its new owners. Menus here feature good local produce cooked in the modern fusion style and featuring predominantly fresh seafood. AA 3 Stars. STB 3 Star.

MELVICH

Bighouse Lodge
Melvich
Sutherland
KW14 7YJ
Tel 01641 531207
Fax 01641 531207
email ackaywares@bighouselodge.co.uk
Web www.bighouselodge.co.uk

Bighouse Lodge is a wonderful traditional Highland Shooting lodge which is now a highly exclusive small hotel. The standards here are exceptionally high, from the comfort and service to the superb meals which are cooked and presented with great style.

MILNGAVIE

Gingerhill
1 Hillhead Street
Milngavie G62 8AF
Tel 0141 956 6515
Fax 0141 956 6515
Web www.gingerhill.co.uk

Situated within the shopping precinct in Milngavie, Gingerhill is a restaurant which has established a style which is both informal and contemporary. The cooking here is highly professional and menus are innovative and well-balanced.

MOFFAT

Lime Tree Restaurant
High Street
Moffat
DG10 9HG
Tel 01683 221654
Fax 01683 221721
Web www.limetree-restaurant.co.uk

The Limetree Restaurant is another of these superb restaurants in Scotland where you can be assured of the highest standard of culinary experience. The Chef demonstrates a considerable array of skills in preparing menus and meals which are a delight.

MOFFAT

The Weavers Restaurant
Moffat Woollen Mill
Ladyknowe
Moffat
Dumfriesshire DG10 9ED
Tel 01683 220134
Fax 01683 221066
email mofftwm499@ewm.co.uk

The Moffat Woollen Mill has an attractive self-service restaurant which serves a range of dishes from tasty home bakes to snacks and light meals all of which make good use of local produce in relaxing surroundings.

MOFFAT

Well View Hotel
Ballplay Road
Moffat
DG10 9JH
Tel 01683 220184
Fax 01683 220088
email info@wellview.co.uk
Web www.wellview.co.uk

Well View Hotel is run by Janet and John Schuckardt who are accomplished and experienced hosts. Janet's cooking is highly regarded and she only uses the very best of local produce which is always beautifully cooked and presented.

MUIR OF ORD

Ord House Hotel
Muir of Ord
Ross-shire IV6 7UH
Tel 01463 870492
Fax 01463 870492
email admin@ord-house.co.uk

Web www.ord-house.co.uk

This 17th Century House has been expertly run by Eliza Allen for years. It is a comfortable and relaxing home which has recently undergone the refurbishment of the main rooms in the hotel. Eliza's cooking is superb, using good local produce which is prepared with imagination and some subtle modern touches. AA Rosette

MULL, ISLE OF

The Dovecote Restaurant
Calgary Hotel
by Dervaig
Isle of Mull
PA75 6QW
Tel 01688 400256
Fax 01688 400256
email calgary.farmhouse@virgin.net
Web www.calgary.co.uk

Calgary Hotel is composed of tastefully refurbished farm buildings containing rustic furnishings to create a charming environment. This is a popular place with locals and particularly families as children are most welcome. The cooking is of an excellent standard, produce all locally-sourced, and the atmosphere is friendly and informal.

MULL, ISLE OF

Druimard Country House
Dervaig
Isle of Mull
PA75 6QW
Tel 01688 400345
Fax 01688 400345
email druimard.hotel@virgin.net
Web www.druimard.co.uk

Druimard is an supremely welcoming small hotel set in attractive gardens. The service is attentive and the cooking is skilled and carefully executed. A particularly well-run family hotel.

MULL, ISLE OF

Druimnacroish Hotel
Dervaig
Isle of Mull PA75 6QW
Tel 01688 400274
Fax 01688 400274
email taste@druimnacroish.co.uk
Web www.druimnacroish.co.uk

Druimnacroish is centrally located on Mull and therefore serves as an ideal base for touring the island. It has a relaxing and informal ambience and the cooking here is of a good standard using much local produce.

MULL, ISLE OF

Gruline Home Farm
Gruline
Isle of Mull
PA71 6HR
Tel 01680 300581
Fax 01680 300573
email boo@gruline.com
Web www.gruline.com

Gruline Home Farm is a small and friendly Bed and Breakfast establishment. The standards here are exceptionally high in this welcoming family home and the cooking is superb.

MULL, ISLE OF

Highland Cottage
Breadalbane Street
Tobermory
Isle of Mull
PH75 6PD
Tel 01688 302030
email david&jo@highlandcottage.co.uk
Web www.highlandcottage.co.uk

Highland Cottage is a luxuriously appointed small hotel which overlooks Tobermory Bay. David and Jo Currie are accomplished hosts who have quickly established exceptional levels of service and cooking in the relatively short time they have been in operation. The food here is highly accomplished, service attentive and friendly – a very special place indeed. Thistle Award Hotel of the Year 2001. AA Top 200. 2 AA Rosettes.

MULL, ISLE OF

The Old Byre Heritage Centre
The Old Byre
Dervaig
Isle of Mull
PA75 6QR
Tel 01688 400229
email theoldbyre@lineone.net

The Old Byre Heritage Centre is a converted byre tearoom where you can be sure of a good range of home baking, home-made soups and light snacks. This is a relaxed and informal place which also has a fascinating range of local crafts for sale.

MULL, ISLE OF

The Water's Edge Restaurant
The Tobermory Hotel
Main Street
Tobermory
Isle of Mull
PA75 6NT
Tel 01688 302091
Fax 01688 302254
email tobhotel@tinyworld.co.uk
Web www.thetobermoryhotel.com

The Water's Edge Restaurant in the Tobermory Hotel is an excellent venue to enjoy well-crafted Scottish cooking using locally-sourced produce. This is set right on the front of the harbour and has achieved a successful blend of friendly service and delicious food in comfortable surroundings.

NAIRN

Boath House
Auldearn, Nairn
Inverness-shire IV12 5TE
Tel 01667 454896
email wendy@boath-house.demon.co.uk

Boath House is a jewel in the Highland crown. Wendy and Don Matheson are the consummate hosts and the house is both elegant and charming. The menus are inspiring – and the meals are outstanding – prepared by an experienced and skilled Chef.

NAIRN

Cawdor Tavern
Cawdor
Nairn IV12 5XP
Tel 01667 404777
Fax 01667 404777
Web www.cawdortavern.com

Cawdor Tavern is a popular and busy pub where you can enjoy an outstanding bar meal or a more formal dining experience in the restaurant. Either way, the food is freshly prepared and of an exceptional standard.

NAIRN

The Golf View Hotel & Leisure Club
The Seafront
Nairn IV12 4HD
Tel 01667 452301
Fax 01667 455267
email rooms@morton-hotels.com
Web www.morton-hotels.com

The Golf View is a popular hotel in a delightful location, with superb views and excellent facilities. Here you can be sure of good Highland hospitality, excellent service and a high standard of meals prepared using local produce by an experienced, professional team.

NAIRN

The Newton Hotel & Highland Conference Centre
Inverness Road
Nairn
IV12 4RX
Tel 01667 453144
Fax 01667 454026
email rooms@morton-hotels.com
Web www.morton-hotels.com

The Newton Hotel is situated on the outskirts of Nairn. The Conference Centre has excellent facilities making it a popular choice for a wide range of events. The menus here are modern Scottish and the cooking is first rate, using only local produce in an imaginative way.

NAIRN

Sunny Brae Hotel
Marine Road
Nairn IV12 4EA
Tel 01667 452309
Fax 01667 454860
email tos@sunnybraehotel.com
Web www.sunnybraehotel.com

Sylvia and Ian Bochel – who own and run Sunnybrae Hotel – are welcoming and sensitive hosts. The hotel has stunning views over the Moray Firth and is very comfortable place to base yourself. The cooking here is excellent – using quality local produce which is prepared with flair and presented with panache.

NEWBURGH

Udny Arms Hotel
Main Street
Newburgh
Aberdeenshire
AB41 6BB
Tel 01358 789444
Fax 01358 789012
email enquiry@udny.demon.co.uk
Web www.udny.co.uk

Udny Arms is rightly popular with locals and visitors. It's a comfortable traditional hotel which achieves exemplary standards of food in both bar and restaurant – both menus featuring local produce which is expertly prepared and presented.

NEWTON STEWART

Corsemalzie House Hotel
Port William
Newton Stewart
DG8 9RL
Tel 01988 860254
email corsemalzie@ndirect.co.uk
Web www.corsemalzie-house.ltd.uk

Corsemalzie is a delightful 19th Century country mansion. This is a grand and welcoming hotel and the delicious meals served in the restaurant combine classic country house style with some modern innovations.

NEWTON STEWART

Kirroughtree House
Newton Stewart
DG8 6AN
Tel 01671 402141
Fax 01671 402425
email info@kirroughtreehouse.co.uk
Web www.mcmillanhotels.com

Kirroughtree is a stunning building, home to an elegant hotel which offers guests an experience to relish. The menus are inspiring, the cooking complements the high standard of the surroundings.

NEWTON STEWART

Marrbury Smokehouse
The Orangerie at Marrbury
Bargrennan
Newton Stewart
Dumfries & Galloway
DG8 6RW
Tel 01671 840241
Fax 01671 840241
email marrbury@hotmail.com

Marrbury Smokehouse has an attractive coffee shop which not only serves a high standard of home bakes and light meals but also is an excellent place to purchase some of the excellent smoked produce.

NEWTONGRANGE

The Scottish Mining Museum
Lady Victoria Colliery, Newtongrange
Midlothian EH22 4QA
Tel 0131 663 7519
Fax 0131 654 1618
email director@
scottishminingmuseum.com
Web www.scottishminingmuseum.com

The coffee shop at the Scottish Mining Museum has a tempting range of dishes from light snacks to more substantial meals and is open all day. It's an interesting venue in its own right and well worth a visit.

NORTH BERWICK

The Scottish Seabird Centre
The Harbour, North Berwick
East Lothian EH39 4SS
Tel 01620 890202
Fax 01620 890222
email info@seabird.org
Web www.seabird.org

The Scottish Seabird Centre is an award-winning visitor attraction which has much to offer all ages and tastes. The menu in the café has a selection of dishes from home baking to light snacks and more substantial meals – all skilfully prepared and presented using local produce.

NORTH CONNEL

Blarcreen Farm Guest House
Ardchattan
North Connel
Nr Oban PA37 1RG
Tel 01631 750272
Fax 01631 750272
email
j.lace@blarcreenfarm.demon.co.uk/
reservations@blarcreenfarm.com
Web www.blarcreenfarm.com

Blarcreen Farm Guest House is set in beautiful Argyll countryside with pleasant gardens. The house is very comfortable and hostess Joanna Lace-

Devere is an accomplished cook who prepares and presents quite exceptional meals for her guests' enjoyment.

NORTH UIST, ISLE OF

Langass Lodge
Langass
Isle of North Uist
The Western Isles HS6 5HA
Tel 01876 580285
Fax 01876 580385
email langasslodge@btconnect.com
Web www.langasslodge.co.uk

Langass Lodge is a very pleasant country house set in a delightful remote location. The standards of service and comfort here are very high and the hosts are welcoming and attentive. Cooking is very good and makes imaginative use of local produce.

OBAN

Barcaldine House Hotel
Barcaldine
By Oban PA37 1SG
Tel 01631 720219
email barcaldine@breathe.co.uk
Web www.countrymansions.com

Barcaldine House Hotel is an elegant, small country house hotel located on the outskirts of Oban. This is a very relaxing place to stay in a fine setting. The cooking is of an excellent standard, good local produce handled with care.

OBAN

The Barn
Cologin, Lerags
By Oban PA34 4SE
Tel 01631 564618

The Barn is a popular country pub located in an isolated spot but worth seeking out. The food here is good honest pub fare which features Scottish produce particularly on the daily changing blackboard.

OBAN

Ee'usk
North Pier
Oban
Argyll PA34 5QD
Tel 01631 565666

There are now two Ee'usk Restaurants – both are superb fish restaurants – one is located in the centre of Oban and the other on the North Pier with the most superb views of the bay. These are stylish yet simply presented restaurants where the speciality is most emphatically locally-sourced seafood. The service is friendly and the cooking is skilled. Either is a great choice to enjoy the best the West Coast has to offer.

OBAN

The Gathering Restaurant and O'Donnells Irish Bar
Breadalbane Street
Oban PA34 5NZ
Tel 01631 565421/564849/566159
Fax 01631 565421
email gatheringoban@aol.com

The Gathering Restaurant and O'Donnells Irish Bar are located right in the town centre and are popular with visitors and locals. It's an informal place to enjoy simple, well-prepared local food in convivial surroundings.

OBAN

Isle of Eriska Hotel
Ledaig, by Oban
Argyll PA37 1SD
Tel 01631 720371
email beppo@eriska-hotel.co.uk

Eriska is one very special place. On its own island and set in beautiful grounds, this family-run country house hotel sets very high standards. The house is beautifully maintained and elegant with cooking to match – classic and carefully presented.

OBAN

Lerags House
Lerags, Oban
Argyll PA34 4SE
Tel 01631 563381
email eat@leragshouse.com
Web www.leragshouse.com

Lerags House is a lovely country house where guests may enjoy a fine experience. The standard of accommodation is good – the cooking is superb and makes best use of the freshest local seafood and produce.

OBAN

Loch Melfort Hotel & Restaurant
Arduaine, by Oban
Argyll PA34 4XG
Tel 01852 200233
Fax 01852 200214
email lmhotel@aol.com
Web www.loch-melfort.co.uk

Loch Melfort Hotel sits on the coast with stunning views of Loch Melfort and Isle of Luing. This hotel is popular with the yachting fraternity as well as locals and other visitors. You have a choice of dining in the hotel or the bistro – both serve excellent local produce, deftly and beautifully presented. 2 AA Rosettes.

OBAN

The Lorne Hotel
Stevenson Street
Oban PA34 5NA
Tel 01631 570020
Fax 01631 562211

The Lorne Hotel is a family-run pub centrally located and rightly popular with locals and visitors. Food here is locally sourced, freshly prepared and simply presented. Good blackboard specials.

OBAN

Manor House
Gallanach Road
Oban
PA34 4LS
Tel 01631 562087
Fax 01631 563053
email manorhouseoban@aol.com
Web www.manorhouseoban.com

The Manor House sit on the hill overlooking Oban Bay. It is a particularly attractive building and guests will find the hotel to be both comfortable and hospitable. The menus here are well balanced and feature much locally sourced produce. The cooking is a skilled balance of traditional and modern Scottish.

OBAN

Willowburn Hotel
Clachan-Seil, by Oban
Argyll PA34 4TJ
Tel 01852 300276
Fax 01852 300597
email willowburn.hotel@virgin.net
Web www.willowburn.co.uk

Willowburn is located just over the 'Atlantic Bridge' on Seil Island. It is a delightful small hotel run by welcoming and accomplished hosts. The food is all expertly prepared on site and features fresh local produce in interesting and appealing menus.

OBAN

Yacht Corryvreckan
Dal an Eas, Kilmore
Oban
Argyll PA34 4XU
Tel 01631 770246
Fax 01631 770246
email yacht.corryvreckan@virgin.net
Web www.corryvreckan.co.uk

Yacht Corryvreckan offers a unique experience for those who love the sea and good food. Douglas and Mary Lindsay are a great team who make their guests most welcome. The cooking is outstanding, from home-made scones to the freshly (very freshly!) prepared seafood.

ONICH, BY FORT WILLIAM

Four Seasons Bistro & Bar
Inchree, Onich
by Fort William PH33 6SE
Tel 01855 821393
Fax 01855 821287
email enquiry@restaurant-scotland.com
Web www.restaurant-scotland.com

Four Seasons Bistro and Bar is a timber-built bar and restaurant set half a mile from the main road. This is a cosy and welcoming rustic place where the very best of local produce is presented in friendly informal surroundings.

ONICH, BY FORT WILLIAM

Lochside Restaurant
The Lodge On The Loch Hotel
Onich, by Fort William
The Scottish Highlands PH33 6RY
Tel 01871 2223462
Fax 01871 2223463

email reservations@freedomglen.co.uk
Web www.freedomglen.co.uk

The Lodge on the Loch Hotel is a pleasant small hotel with lovely lochside views. The interior of the hotel is unique and tasteful and the menus are an interesting combination of international influences and superb local produce, adroitly prepared and presented. 2 AA Rosettes

ORKNEY

Balfour Castle
Shapinsay
Orkney
KW17 2DY
Tel 01856 711282
Fax 01856 711283
email balfourcastle@btinternet.com
Web www.balfourcastle.co.uk

Balfour Castle is unique, and only a two-minute walk from the Shapinsay ferry. The hotel is very comfortable and the cooking uses only local produce – it's all home made and the standards are high.

ORKNEY

Cleaton House Hotel
Westray
Orkney
KW17 2DB
Tel 01857 677508
Fax 01857 677442
email cleaton@orkney.com
Web www.cleatonhouse.com

Cleaton House is located on the island of Westray which should be on everyone's itinerary of the Orkneys. The hotel is superbly run and accommodation is delightful. The menus feature Orcadian produce which is simply but subtly prepared and presented.

The Creel Restaurant
Front Road, St Margarets Hope
South Ronaldsay
Orkney KW17 2SL
Tel 01856 831311
email alan@thecreel.freeserve.co.uk
Web www.thecreel.com

The Creel is a front runner for the best
places to eat in Orkney. Run by Joyce and
Alan Craigie, this small restaurant has
been rightly recognised for the consistently
high standard and innovative use of
Orcadian produce. Not to be missed.

Ferry Inn
10 John Street, Stromness
Orkney KW16 3AD
Tel 01856 850280
Fax 01856 851332
email advian@ferryinn.com
Web www.ferryinn.com

The Ferry Inn is a popular and lively inn
where great local Orcadian produce
always features and where you are sure

of a warm welcome. Good food, simple
prepared and presented.

Foveran Hotel & Restaurant
St Ola, Kirkwall
Orkney KW15 1SF
Tel 01856 872389
Fax 01856 876430
email foveranhotel@aol.com
Web www.foveranhotel.co.uk

Foveran Hotel is run by the Doull family
whose commitment to offering a
genuine Orcadian welcome, hospitality
and cooking is gaining them a growing
and justified reputation. A very
convenient place to base yourself
whilst exploring all the wonders of
Orkney! Taste of Orkney Food Awards.

ORKNEY

Hamnavoe Restaurant
Graham Place, Stromness
Orkney
Tel 01856 850606

The Hamnavoe Restaurant offers a genuine Orcadian welcome and a pleasing menu which offers a good range of local produce – skillfully prepared and presented. Winner Taste of Orkney 2004 Best Evening Meal.

ORKNEY

Julia's Café & Bistro
Ferry Road, Stromness
Orkney
Tel 01856 850904

Julia's Café & Bistro is centrally located in Stromness and is a superb place to enjoy good Orcadian produce, freshly prepared and presented, in informal and welcoming surroundings. Winner Taste of Orkney Best Lunch/High Tea.

ORKNEY

The Kirkwall Hotel
Harbour Street
Kirkwall
Orkney KW15 1LF
Tel 01856 872232
Fax 01856 872812
email enquiries@kirkwallhotel.com
Web www.kirkwallhotel.com

The Kirkwall Hotel is a fine Victorian building and is the largest of Orkney's hotels. It is pleasantly situated on the seafront with superb views. The welcome is genuine and the cooking is good fresh local produce skillfully prepared and presented.

ORKNEY

Lav'rockha Guest House
Inganess Road
Orkney
KW15 1SP
Tel 01856 876103
Fax 01856 876103
email lavrockha@orkney.com
Web www.lavrockha.co.uk

Lav'rockha is a modern and very comfortable guest house on the edge of Kirkwall. The welcome here is exceptional, the hospitality excellent and the home cooking taking in imaginative use of local produce.

ORKNEY

The Orkney Hotel
40 Victoria Street
Kirkwall
Orkney KW15 1DN
Tel 01856 873477
Fax 01856 872767
email info@orkneyhotel.co.uk
Web www.orkneyhotel.co.uk

The Orkney Hotel is a popular meeting place, centrally located in Kirkwall. The hotel is comfortable and the food here is excellent, featuring local produce with a wide selection to suit all tastes.

ORKNEY

The Sands Hotel
Burray
Orkney
Tel 01856 731298

The Sands Hotel specialises in locally landed fish and shellfish all of which feature daily. Here you may also enjoy prime Orkney beef cooked to taste with delicious homemade desserts to follow in warm and welcoming surroundings.

ORKNEY

Woodwick House
Evie
Orkney KW17 2PQ
Tel 01856 751330
Fax 01856 751383
email mail@woodwickhouse.co.uk
Web www.woodwickhouse.co.uk

Woodwick House is a relaxing and peaceful small hotel. It has a genuine farmhouse feel to it and is very welcoming. The cooking here is simple but effective, with extensive use of the superb local produce.

PALNACKIE

The Crows Nest
Glen Road, Palnackie
Dumfries and Galloway DG7 1PH
Tel 01556 600217
email thecrowsnest@totalise.co.uk

At the Crows Nest, you're bound to find something from a menu which has something to suit everyone. It is a popular and informal restaurant which is open all day and serves a fine range of snacks and meals all freshly prepared and efficiently presented.

PEAT INN

The Peat Inn
Peat Inn
by Cupar
Fife KY15 5LH
Tel 01334 840206
Fax 01334 840530
email reception@thepeatinn.co.uk
Web www.thepeatinn.co.uk

The Peat Inn has a justifiable reputation for consistently high quality in a very attractive setting. David Wilson has been something of a pioneer of the use of the best fresh Scottish produce and is a distinguished and innovative Chef. A very special place indeed.

PEEBLES

Castle Venlaw Hotel
Edinburgh Road
Peebles EH45 8QG
Tel 01721 720384
Fax 01721 724066
email stay@venlaw.co.uk
Web www.venlaw.co.uk

Castle Venlaw is a superb hotel set in beautiful grounds. The welcome here is genuine and the standard of cooking is excellent. Menus are innovative and feature the best of local produce, dexterously prepared. 2 AA Rosettes. Good Hotel Guide.

PEEBLES

Cringletie House
Edinburgh Road
Peebles EH45 8PL
Tel 01721 725750
Fax 01721 725751
email enquiries@cringletie.com
Web www.cringletie.com

Cringletie House is set in 28 acres of beautiful grounds and woodland and is a very comfortable and charming hotel. The cooking is highly skilled and makes excellent use of local produce, and the wine list is extensive. Owners Jacob and Johanna will ensure that your stay is memorable. AA 2 Rosettes. Winner Best Restaurant Meal of the Borders 2003.

NEAR PENICUIK

Howgate Restaurant
Howgate, Nr Penicuik
Midlothian EH26 8PY
Tel 01968 670000
email info@howgate.com
Web www.howgate.com

The Howgate Restaurant is a beautifully renovated restaurant near Penicuik on the outskirts of Edinburgh. Here you may dine in the bistro or the restaurant – either way the standard of menu and cooking skills is excellent. Service is attentive and friendly.

PERTH

63 Tay Street Restaurant
63 Tay Street
Perth PH2 8NN
Tel 01738 441451
Fax 01738 441461

63 Tay Street is an excellent restaurant and has been rightly recognised for the quality of the cooking and excellent service. Shona and Jeremy Wares are experienced and enthusiastic and this is demonstrated from the tempting menus and warm welcome. A very skilful and talented team.

PERTH

Ballathie House Hotel
Kinclaven, by Stanley
Perth
Perthshire PH1 4QN

Tel 01250 883268
Fax 01250 883396
email mail@ballathiehousehotel.com
Web www.ballathiehousehotel.com

Ballathie is a relaxing and delightful country house which is set on the River Tay. You may dine here in the bar or restaurant – whichever you choose, you are assured of the most inviting menus, excellent local produce, cooked and presented with the deftest of touches. A great favourite for locals and visitors alike.

PERTH

Exceed Restaurant
35/37 Main Street
Bridgend
Perth
PH2 7HD
Tel 01738 626000
email exceed@bt.connect.com

Exceed is another establishment run by Willie Little – the other being Cargills in Blairgowrie. Perth boasts a number of very good restaurants and this is certainly one of them. Stylish food, imaginatively prepared and served in stylish surroundings by friendly and efficient staff.

PERTH

Huntingtower Hotel
Crieff Road
Perth PH1 3JT
Tel 01738 583771
Fax 01738 583777
email reservations@
huntingtowerhotel.co.uk
Web www.huntingtowerhotel.co.uk

You'll find Huntingtower Hotel just on the outskirts of Perth. This is a tastefully renovated hotel which is set in beautiful grounds. The service is warm and attentive and the cooking is based around good local produce, prepared and presented with considerable style.

PERTH

Kinfauns Castle
Dundee Road
Perth
Tel 01738 620777

Kinfauns Castle on the outskirts of Perth is a unique hotel in an elevated setting. The building has been tastefully and luxuriously appointed. The cooking is of a consistently high standard, ably presented and featuring good quality local produce.

PERTH

Let's Eat
77 Kinnoull Street
Perth
PH1 5EZ
Tel 01738 643377
Fax 01738 621464
email shona@letseatperth.co.uk
Web www.letseatperth.co.uk

Let's Eat is a very popular restaurant in Perth and with good reason. Tony Heath is a gifted and imaginative Chef who sets the highest standards and achieves them. Shona is a welcoming and chamring host – between them they have created a successful recipe for superb dining in comfortable and relaxed surroundings.

PERTH

Macmillan Coffee Shop
Quarrymill Woodland Park
Isla Road
Perth
PH2 7HQ
Tel 01738 633890
email Ann.F.Alexander@btinternet.com

This unique coffee shop is run by volunteers – all proceeds are donated to cancer relief. Not surprisingly, it's become a popular place to enjoy good home baking or snacks in friendly surroundings.

PERTH

Café 22
The New County Hotel
22-30 County Place
Perth PH2 8EE
Tel 01738 623355
Fax 01738 628969
email enquiries@newcountyhotel.com
Web www.newcountyhotel.com

The New County Hotel has Café 22 – an excellent tearoom serving a superb range of home baking, snacks and light meals in comfortable, friendly and informal surroundings.

PERTH

Acanthus Restaurant
Parklands Hotel
2 St Leonards Bank
Perth PH2 8EB
Tel 01738 622451
Fax 01738 622046
email parklands.perth@virgin.net
Web www.parklandshotelperth.com

Parklands is a comfortable and elegant hotel which offers a high standard of accommodation and facilities. You may dine in the bistro or the more formal restaurant – menus are rewarding and the food is very good.

PERTH

The Perth Theatre Restaurant Café & The Lang Bar
185 High Street
Perth PH1 5UW
Tel 01738 472709
Fax 01738 624576
email phood@perththeatre.co.uk
Web www.perththeatre.co.uk

Perth Theatre is a popular venue for theatre-goers and its menus are prepared with imagination, skill and humour – you'll find they are themed depending upon the production being staged at the time. All produce is local at this consistently good establishment.

PERTH

Perthshire Visitor Centre
Bankfoot
Perth
PH1 4EB
Tel 01738 787696
Fax 01738 787120
email calum@macbeth.co.uk
Web www.macbeth.co.uk

The Perthshire Visitor Centre is a fine restaurant and conservatory with ample parking and plenty for all ages to see. The food here reflects the high quality of the local produce used, and menus have something to suit all tastes and times of day. 4 Star Tourist Shop

PITLOCHRY

Donavourd House Hotel
Lily's Restaurant
Pitlochry PH16 5JS
Tel 01796 472100
email reservations@
donavourdhousehotel.co.uk
Web www.donavourdhousehotel.co.uk

Donavourd is an attractive and very comfortable small hotel run by accomplished and welcoming hosts. The cooking here is of a modern Scottish style, all freshly prepared and innovatively presented with dexterity and flair.

PITLOCHRY

East Haugh Country House Hotel
Pitlochry
Perthshire
PH16 5TE
Tel 01796 473121

Fax 01796 472473
email easthaugh@aol.com

East Haugh is a lovely family-owned and run hotel. The accommodation is both comfortable and thoughtfully furnished. Meals can be enjoyed in the conservatory bar and restaurant and are prepared with professionalism and presented with flair. STB 4 Star Small Hotel

PITLOCHRY

The Green Park Hotel
Clunie Bridge Road
Pitlochry
PH16 5JY
Tel 01796 473248
Fax 01796 473520
email bookings@thegreenpark.co.uk
Web www.thegreenpark.co.uk

Comfortable and relaxing, the Green Park Hotel occupies an idyllic location overlooking Loch Faskally. The accommodation is of a very high standard, as is the food – good local produce prepared and presented in Scottish traditional style with flair.

PITLOCHRY

Killiecrankie Hotel
Killiecrankie
by Pitlochry
PH16 5LG
Tel 01796 473220
Fax 01796 472451
email enquiries@killiecrankiehotel.co.uk
Web www.killiecrankiehotel.co.uk

The Killiecrankie Hotel is a well-appointed and well-run small hotel. The accommodation is finished to a very high standard and the service is attentive and friendly. Menus all use the best local produce and the cooking is highly proficient and beautifully presented.

PITLOCHRY

Knockendarroch House Hotel
Higher Oakfield
Pitlochry
PH16 5HT
Tel 01796 473473
Fax 01796 474068
email info@knockendarroch.co.uk
Web www.knockendarroch.co.uk

Knockendarroch House is a relaxed family hotel run by accomplished and welcoming hosts. The standard of accommodation is excellent and the views are superb. Here you will enjoy a superb dining experience in the traditional manner, in keeping with the surroundings and using only excellent local produce.

PITLOCHRY

Moulin Inn
11 Kirkmichael Road
Pitlochry
PH16 5EH
Tel 01796 472196

The Moulin Inn is a well-known and popular inn in this busy Perthshire town. The bar is a comfortable and friendly place with an informal ambience. It serves good pub food featuring local produce, expertly cooked and presented.

PITLOCHRY

The Old Armoury
Armoury Road
Pitlochry
Perthshire
PH16 5AP
Tel 01796 474281
Fax 01796 473157
email angus@
theoldarmouryrestaurant.fsnet.co.uk

The Old Armoury is a delight. This small and very welcoming restaurant is run by accomplished and hospitable hosts. The menus here are innovative and the service attentive. Memorable food in delightful surroundings.

PITLOCHRY

The Pitlochry Festival Theatre Restaurant
Port-na-Craig
Pitlochry
PH16 5DR
Tel 01796 484600
Fax 01796 484616
email admin@pitlochry.org.uk
Web www.pitlochry.org.uk

Pitlochry Festival Theatre has something to offer everyone, not just theatre-goers. The restaurant serves good food and menus change frequently and uses all locally-sourced produce.

PLOCKTON

The Haven Hotel
Plockton
Ross-shire IV52 8TW
Tel 01599 544223/334
Fax 01599 544467
Web www.smoothhound.co.uk/
hotels/thehaven.html

The Haven Hotel is a small, traditional family-run hotel in this pretty Highland village. Menus are innovative and the cooking is very professional. A friendly and welcoming spot to enjoy good food while exploring the surrounding area.

PLOCKTON

The Plockton Hotel
Harbour Street, Plockton
Ross-shire IV52 8TN
Tel 01599 544274
Fax 01599 544475
email info@plocktonhotel.co.uk
Web www.plocktonhotel.co.uk

The Plockton Hotel is set on the seafront and is a very comfortable and tastefully furnished hotel. The cooking here is superb – great fresh local produce with menus to suit every taste. Their small garden is a delight on a sunny day!

POLMONT

Macdonald Inchyra Hotel
Grange Road
Polmont
Falkirk FK2 0YB
email info@
inchyra-macdonald-hotels.co.uk

The Macdonald Inchyra Hotel is a large and popular meeting place and venue. The accommodation is superior and the facilities first rate. There is a range of dining options here – right through from informal to formal dining. The standard is high throughout and there is an emphasis on fresh, locally-sourced ingredients.

POOLEWE

Inverewe Garden Restaurant
Poolewe
Ross-shire
IV22 2LG
Tel 01445 781446
Fax 01445 781446
email ddonald@nts.org.uk
Web www.nts.org.uk

Inverewe Garden Restaurant is another fine National Trust for Scotland property set beside one of the most beautiful gardens in Scotland. The self-service restaurant offers a mouth-watering variety of freshly prepared snacks and light meals and a wide range of excellent home baking.

POOLEWE

Pool House
Poolewe
by Inverewe Gardens
Wester Ross
IV22 2LD
Tel 01445 781272
Fax 01445 781403
email enquiries@poolhousehotel.com
Web www.poolhousehotel.com

Pool House Hotel is one of the finest places to stay and dine in this part of the west coast. The accommodation is of a very high standard, hospitality is welcoming and the standard of cooking complements the quality of ingredients and surroundings. 3 AA Red Stars. 2 Rosettes

PORT APPIN

The Airds Hotel
Port Appin
Argyll PA38 4DF
Tel 01631 730236
Fax 01631 730535
email airds@airds-hotel.com
Web www.airds-hotel.com

Airds Hotel has always had a superb
reputation – and this is being
maintained under its new owners. It is
in a delightful setting – very
comfortable accommodation and
excellent service. The cooking remains
of a very high standard too, using much
of the abundant, high quality produce
available locally.

PORT OF MENTEITH

The Lake Hotel
Port of Menteith
Perthshire
FK8 3PA
Tel 01877 385258
Fax 01877 385671
email enquiries@
lake-of-menteith-hotel.com
Web www.lake-of-menteith-hotel.com

Sitting on the shore of Scotland's only
lake, the Lake of Menteith Hotel is a
most elegant and comfortable hotel
where you can enjoy good food in a
very pleasant setting.

PORTPATRICK

Mariner Restaurant
Downshire Arms Hotel
Main Street
Portpatrick
By Stranraer
DG9 8JJ
Tel 01776 810300
Fax 01776 810620
email downshirearmshotel@mail.com
Web www.downshirearmshotel.net

The Downshire Arms is a comfortable
small hotel set in this delightful

village. Local Galloway produce
features prominently on the menus
here and is well cooked and
attractively presented.

PORTPATRICK

Knockinaam Lodge
Portpatrick
DG9 9AD
Tel 01776 810471
Fax 01776 810435
email reservations@
knockinaamlodge.com
Web www.knockinaamlodge.com

Knockinaam Lodge is a beautiful and
stylish small country house hotel in a
quite unique setting – how many hotels
can boast having their very own beach?
The accommodation is comfortable and
dining here is a special experience,
highly-skilled modern Scottish cooking
which is presented with flair.

PRESTWICK

Parkstone Hotel
Central Esplanade
Prestwick
Ayrshire
KA9 1QN
Tel 01292 477286
Fax 01292 477671
email info@parkstonehotel.co.uk
Web www.parkstonehotel.co.uk

Parkstone Hotel is a charming seafront
hotel, looking out over the Clyde. It is
welcoming and friendly and the food is
excellent, menus reflect local produce,
are well balanced and the cooking is
exceptional.

SCONE

Old Masters Restaurant
Murrayshall House Hotel
Scone
Nr Perth PH2 7PH
Tel 01738 551171
Fax 01738 552595
email lin.murrayshall@virgin.net
Web www.murrayshall.com

Located just a few minutes out of
Perth, Murrayshall Hotel is situated in
its own grounds with excellent
facilities. It's a comfortable and relaxing
hotel which also has well-appointed
lodges in the grounds. The cooking
here is first rate and there are several
dining options, all of which make good
use of fresh local produce.

SELKIRK

Philipburn House Hotel
Selkirk TD7 5LS
Tel 01750 20747
Fax 01750 21690
email info@philipburnhousehotel.co.uk
Web www.philipburnhousehotel.co.uk

An extremely comfortable place to stay,
Philipburn House Hotel's standards are
high throughout. There are several
dining options here but all have in
common the commitment to local
produce which is skilfully prepared and
beautifully presented.

SHETLAND

Almara
Upper Urafirth, Hillswick
Shetland ZE2 9RH
Tel 01806 503261

Fax 01806 503261
email almara@zetnet.co.uk
Web www.users.zetnet.co.uk/almara

Marcia Williamson is a warm and
welcoming hostess. Almara is a
supremely comfortable house where
guests can enjoy the true flavour of
Shetland with the highest quality
cuisine featuring good local produce and
cooked and presented simply with style.

SHETLAND

Busta House Hotel
Busta, Brae
Shetland ZE2 9QN
Tel 01806 522 506
Fax 01806 522 588
email reservations@bustahouse.com
Web www.bustahouse.com

Busta House is an historic building and an
ideal place to enjoy Shetland hospitality.
The accommodation is very comfortable
and the service attentive and friendly.
The meals here reflect the high standard
of local produce available and are cooked
and presented with care and flair.

SHETLAND

Monty's Bistro
5 Mounthooly Street, Lerwick
Shetland ZE1 0BJ
Tel 01595 696555
Fax 01595 696955

Monty's Bistro is an excellent, informal
bistro in the town centre. The food here
is superb, the service friendly and the
welcome sincere. Raymond is an inspired
and innovative chef and this is definitely
one place to visit during your stay.

SKYE, ISLE OF

Bosville Hotel
9-10 Bosville Terrace, Portree
Isle of Skye IV51 9DG
Tel 01478 612846
Fax 01478 613434
email bosville@macleodhotels.co.uk
Web www.macleodhotels.co.uk/bosville

The Bosville Hotel is a popular, centrally-located hotel which has been sensitively refurbished to a high standard. The Chandlery Restaurant is an ideal place to enjoy excellent Skye produce which has been carefully prepared and presented by a skilled and accomplished Chef.

SKYE, ISLE OF

Cuillin Hills Hotel
Portree
Isle of Skye IV51 9QU
Tel 01478 612003
Fax 01478 613092
email office@cuillinhills.demon.co.uk
Web www.cuillinhills.demon.co.uk

Cuillin Hills Hotel occupies an elevated position which affords excellent views of the famous mountain range. This is a very comfortable and well-appointed hotel which offers fine dining in its spacious dining room. The cooking is traditional in a classic style whilst using good local produce.

SKYE, ISLE OF

Hotel Eilean Iarmain
Eilean Iarmain, Sleat
Isle of Skye IV43 8QR
Tel 01471 833332

Fax 01471 833275
email bookings@eilean-iarmain.co.uk
Web www.eileaniarmain.co.uk

Hotel Eilean Iarmain, situated in a beautiful location on the Sleat Peninsula, has many special features and comforts which have added to its popularity over the years. The cooking here is of a very high standard and makes excellent use of local produce. Service is warm, friendly and attentive.

SKYE, ISLE OF

Kinloch Lodge
Sleat
Isle of Skye IV43 8QY
Tel 01471 833214
Fax 01471 833277
email kinloch@dial.pipex.com
Web www.kinloch-lodge.co.uk

Lady Claire Macdonald is an accomplished cook; she, her husband and family run Kinloch Lodge with a unique combination of flair and warmth. This is a very welcoming house where guests enjoy a high standard of surroundings and service. The menus are interesting, displaying the passion for local produce and the cooking is of an excellent standard.

SKYE, ISLE OF

Rosedale Hotel
Beaumont Crescent, Portree
Isle of Skye IV51 9DB
Tel 01478 613131
Fax 01478 612531
email rosedalehotelskye@aol.com
Web www.rosedalehotelskye.co.uk

Rosedale Hotel is situated right on

Portree Harbour with its restaurant offering superb views. This is a family-run establishment where welcome and a high standard of hospitality is a priority along with a commitment to good use of local produce. 3 Star STB. 1AA Rosette.

SKYE, ISLE OF

Roskhill House
by Dunvegan
Isle of Skye
IV55 8ZD
Tel 01470 521317
Fax 01470 521761
email stay@roskhill.demon.co.uk
Web www.roskhill.demon.co.uk

Roskhill House is a comfortable guest house not far from Dunvegan. Run by welcoming hosts, here you can enjoy hearty portions of well-cooked traditional tasty meals which are carefully prepared and presented.

SKYE, ISLE OF

Rowan Cottage
9 Glasnakille
by Elgol
Isle of Skye
IV49 9BQ
Tel 01471 866287
Fax 01471 866287
email ruth@rowancottage-skye.co.uk
Web www.rowancottage-skye.co.uk

Rowan Cottage is a renovated croft house near Elgol, a particularly remote and beautiful part of Skye. This is a peaceful and comfortable place to enjoy stunning surroundings and very good cooking using some of the best local produce around.

SKYE, ISLE OF

The Dining Room and
Lochview Conservatory
Skeabost Country House Hotel
Skeabost Bridge
Skye IV51 9NP
Tel 01470 532202

Fax 01470 532454
email reception@
skeabostcountryhouse.com
Web www.skeabostcountryhouse.com

Skeabost is a lovely Victorian House, set in its own splendid grounds which even include its own golf course. The accommodation is comfortable and the hosts welcoming. Meals are freshly prepared and stylishly presented.

SKYE, ISLE OF

Three Chimneys Restaurant and The House Over-By
Colbost
Dunvegan
Isle of Skye
IV55 8ZT
Tel 01470 511258
Fax 01470 511358
email eatandstay@threechimneys.co.uk
Web www.threechimneys.co.uk

Three Chimneys just keeps getting better. Run by Shirley and Eddie and their family/team this is a very special place. If you have the opportunity to stay in the superb rooms do – but book well in advance as they are always busy. If not, no visit to Skye can be considered complete without enjoying the dining experience here – the cooking is second to none, the produce first class and the passion always in evidence. AA Wine Award for Scotland 2004, 3 AA Rosettes, VisitScotland 5 Star Restaurant with Rooms.

SKYE, ISLE OF

Viewfield House
Portree
Isle of Skye IV51 9EU
Tel 01478 612217
Fax 01478 613517
email info@viewfieldhouse.com
Web www.viewfieldhouse.com

Viewfield House is an impressive Victorian house which has been in the Macdonald family for generations. The dining experience here is excellent – skilled modern Scottish cooking which is served in an impressive Victorian dining room.

SOUTH QUEENSFERRY

Adam Stables Tearoom
Heritage Hospitality Ltd
Hopetoun House
South Queensferry EH30 9SL
Tel 0131 331 4305

Adam Stables Tearoom is an excellent tearoom located within Hopetoun House. The food includes an extensive range of home baking, light snacks and super sandwiches and other home-made dishes. A fine example of high standards of good local produce and friendly service in lovely surroundings.

SOUTH UIST, ISLE OF

Orasay Inn
Lochcarnan
Isle of South Uist
Western Isles HS8 5PD
Tel 01870 610298
Fax 01870 610267
email orasayinn@btinternet.com
Web www.witb.co.uk/links/orasayinn.htm

Orasay Inn is a simple yet charming restaurant which is run by welcoming hosts. The cooking is of a high standard where fresh local produce is simply prepared and presented with flair to allow the flavours speak for themselves.

SPEAN BRIDGE

Corriechoille Lodge
Spean Bridge
Inverness-shire PH34 4EY
Tel 01397 712002
Fax 01397 712002
email mail@corriechoille.co.uk
Web www.corriechoille.com

Corriechoille Lodge is in a gorgeous location with stunning mountain views. The lodge is furnished to a high standard and is a comfortable and welcoming place to stay. The meals here are beautifully prepared and make imaginative use of local produce.

SPEAN BRIDGE

Corriegour Lodge Hotel
Drew's, Loch Lochy
By Spean Bridge PH34 4EB
Tel 01397 712685
Fax 01397 712696
email Info@corriegour-lodge-hotel.com
Web www.corriegour-lodge-hotel.com

Corriegour Lodge Hotel is a small, family-run hotel in a beautiful location. The accommodation is as comfortable as the welcome is sincere. Menus here are innovative, cooking highly skilled and presentation stylish.

SPEAN BRIDGE

Old Pines Restaurant with Rooms
Spean Bridge
by Fort William PH34 4EG
Tel 01397 712324
Fax 01397 712433
email goodfood@oldpines.co.uk
Web www.oldpines.co.uk

Old Pines Restaurant with Rooms is run by Imogen and Ken Dalley who are committed to maintaining the high standards of the previous owners. This is a warm, welcoming place, in a wonderful location where you can enjoy the best of Scottish hospitality and cooking.

ST ANDREWS

The Grange Inn
Grange, nr St Andrews
Tel 01334 472670

The Grange Inn is a small, very fine, restaurant just outside St Andrews in open countryside. This is a splendid place where the welcome and service are of a high standard and the cooking of good local produce simply superb.

ST ANDREWS

The Inn at Lathones
By Largoward
St Andrews KY9 1JE
Tel 01334 840494
Fax 01334 840694
email lathones@theinn.co.uk
Web www.theinn.co.uk

The Inn at Lathones is a delightful, family-run inn with excellent accommodation. The food here is superb.

The best of local produce is prepared with skill and presented with flair.

ST ANDREWS

MacGregors
71 Market Street
St Andrews KY16 9NU
Tel 01334 477106
Fax 01334 478900
email ian@sta-co.com
Web www.macgregorsofstandrews.com

MacGregors is a superb coffee shop in the main street in St Andrews. The shop sells an delightful selection of contemporary gifts and cards and upstairs in the coffee shop you can enjoy a wide range of excellent home bakes, light snacks and other well-prepared Scottish dishes.

ST ANDREWS

The Old Course Hotel Golf Resort & Spa
Old Station Road, St Andrews
Fife KY16 9SP
Tel 01334 474371
Fax 01334 477668
email reservations@oldcoursehotel.co.uk
Web www.oldcoursehotel.co.uk

The Old Course Hotel is a fine and elegant hotel, ideally located on the edge of St Andrews and within easy walking distance of the centre of the town. The accommodation here is of superior quality and the facilities excellent. There are several dining options – Sands Bar and Restaurant is an more informal option with an interesting menu to suit all tastes. The Road Hole Grill is where you will find a very high standard of skilfull cooking and presentation in more formal surrounds with spectacular views. 3 AA Rosettes.

ST ANDREWS

Rufflets Country House
Strathkinness Low Road, St Andrews
Fife KY16 9TX
Tel 01334 472594
Fax 01334 478703
email reservations@rufflets.co.uk
Web www.rufflets.co.uk

Located on the outskirts of St Andrews, Rufflets Country House is an elegant and very comfortable hotel where the service and hospitality match the high standards of the surroundings. The dining experience is superb, highly accomplished cooking of good local produce, beautifully presented.

ST ANDREWS

Russell Hotel
26 The Scores
St Andrews KY16 9AS
Tel 01334 473447
Fax 01334 478279
email russellhotel@talk21.com
Web www.russellhotelsstandrews.co.uk

The Russell Hotel is in a superb location overlooking the sea and the Old Course. The hotel is very comfortable and the quality of meals in the bar is exceptional.

ST ANDREWS

St Andrews Links Clubhouse
West Sands Road, St Andrews
Fife KY16 9XL
Tel 01334 466666
Fax 01334 466664

St Andrews Links Clubhouse is a modern, comfortable and tasteful place to enjoy a whole range of good food and drinks. The standards here are high, from the friendly, professional service to the ample and well presented meals.

ST ANDREWS

Seafood Restaurant
St Andrews
Tel 01334 479475

The Seafood Restaurant has a stunning location with uninterrupted sea views. It is run by the Butler family who have already established high standards at the Seafood Restaurant, St Monans. The quality here matches those standards, menus are innovative and the experience memorable.

ST ANDREWS

The Vine Leaf
131 South Street, St Andrews
Tel 01334 477497

The Vine Leaf is centrally located in the town and a popular small restaurant. Chef Proprietor prides himself in a high standard of service which is matched with well-balanced menus and skilful cooking and presentation.

ST BOSWELLS

Buccleuch Arms
St Boswells, Melrose
Roxburghshire TD6 0EW
Tel 01835 822243
Fax 01835 823965
email info@buccleucharmshotel.co.uk
Web www.buccleucharms.co.uk

The Buccleuch Arms is a delightful 16th

Century coaching inn which is ideally situated for a stop whilst in this particularly picturesque part of the Borders. One can choose from dining in the Restaurant or more informally in the bar where the welcome is friendly and the menus feature good locally sourced produce.

ST BOSWELLS

Tweed Restaurant
Dryburgh Abbey Hotel
St Boswells, Melrose TD6 0RQ
Tel 01835 822261
Fax 01835 823945
email enquiries@dryburgh.co.uk
Web www.dryburgh.co.uk

Dryburgh Abbey Hotel is an imposing red sandstone baronial mansion set on banks of the River Tweed. This fine hotel is popular with locals and visitors and sets high standards. The cooking is exemplary and menus reflect the wonderful local produce available.

ST BOSWELLS

Whitehouse
St Boswells
Roxburghshire TD6 0ED
Tel 01573 460343
Fax 01573 460361
email tyrer.whitehouse@lineone.net
Web www.aboutscotland.com/ south/whitehouse.html

Whitehouse is a charming country house with lovely views of the Cheviots. The meals here make the most of the high standard of local produce available and are served in the relaxing dining room.

ST FILLANS

Meall Reamhar Restaurant & Tarken Room
The Four Seasons Hotel
St Fillans
Perthshire PH6 2NF
Tel 01764 685333
Fax 01764 685444
email info@thefourseasonshotel.co.uk
Web www.thefourseasonshotel.co.uk

The Four Seasons Hotel is set in some of the most stunning countryside in Scotland. A very comfortable small hotel, it is welcoming and friendly. There is a range of dining options here – all of which use fine local produce which is prepared in a modern Scottish style.

ST MONAN'S

The Seafood Restaurant
16 West End, St Monan's
Fife KY10 2BX
Tel 01333 730 327
Fax 01333 730327
email info@theseafoodrestaurant.com
Web www.theseafoodrestaurant.com

The Seafood Restaurant is a wonderful place to enjoy the very best of fresh local seafood in superb surroundings. This is a fine restaurant where the commitment to quality is evident and the standards are high. AA Best Seafood Restaurant for Scotland 2003. 2 AA Rosettes.

STIRLING

Olivia's Restaurant
5 Baker Street
Stirling FK8 1BJ
Tel 01786 446277
Fax 01786 446277

Olivia's Restaurant is a small, attractive restaurant centrally located in the old town. Menus here are an eclectic mix of Scottish with Eastern influence and the quality of local produce is clearly evident in the excellent dishes available.

STONEHAVEN

Lairhillock Inn & Crynoch Restaurant at Lairhillock
Netherley
by Stonehaven
Aberdeenshire
AB39 3QS
Tel 01569 730001
Fax 01569 731175
email lairhillock@breathemail.net
Web www.lairhillock.co.uk

The Lairhillock Inn is over 200 years old and is a deservedly popular meeting place for locals and visitors. The standards here are exceptional – whether dining in the bar or the restaurant. Locally-sourced produce is much in use and the dishes are imaginatively prepared and presented.

STRACHUR

The Creggans Inn
Strachur
Argyll
PA27 8BX
Tel 01369 860279
Fax 01369 860637
email info@creggans-inn.co.uk
Web www.creggans-inn.co.uk

The Creggans Inn is a small hotel run by the Robertson family – highly accomplished hosts. It is a good place to stop for lunch or dinner where guests can be assured of only the finest Scottish produce – skilfully prepared and beautifully presented. A must visit whilst exploring the West Coast.

STRANRAER

Corsewall Lighthouse Hotel
Corsewall Point, Kirkholm
Stranraer DG9 0QG
Tel 01776 853220
Fax 01776 854231
email lighthousehotel@btopenworld.com
Web www.lighthousehotel.co.uk

Corsewall Lighthouse offers a unique experience to its guests. This 19th Century lighthouse is now a listed building and has been converted into a very comfortable small hotel – the accommodation has the ring of good taste and quality at every turn. The superb dining experience brings finest local produce into play, prepared and presented with skill and style.

STRATHCARRON

Shore House
Kishorn, Strathcarron
Wester Ross IV54 8XA
Tel 01520 733333
Fax 01520 733333
email taste@shorehouse.co.uk
Web www.shorehouse.co.uk

Shore House is run by accomplished and experienced hosts Maureen and Douglas Gray. The house is exceedingly comfortable and welcoming and is set in a beautiful location. The cooking here is also superb and makes extensive use of local produce. A very special place indeed.

STRATHPEFFER

Museum Coffee Shop
Victorian Railway Station
Strathpeffer
Ross-shire IV14 9DH
Tel 01997 421136
email Heleninmyrtle@aol.com

The Museum Coffee Shop is located in a converted Victorian Railway Station and is an unusual and pleasant place to take a break. Here you can enjoy a super selection of good home baking, light snacks and meals served in a friendly and homely atmosphere.

STRICHEN

The White Horse Hotel & Restaurant
65 High Street
Strichen
near Fraserburgh
Aberdeenshire
AB43 6SQ
Tel 01771 637218
Fax 01771 637940
email info@whhr.co.uk
Web www.whhr.co.uk

The White Horse Hotel and Restaurant is a comfortable small hotel which has a bar and separate restaurant. The menus here are traditionally Scottish and the cooking is of a particularly high standard in both the restaurant and the bar. Under the new ownership of Tony and Wendy Gibbs who have retained the same staff and plan to upgrade facilities and menus.

STRONTIAN

Kilcamb Lodge Hotel
Strontian
Argyll
PH36 4HY
Tel 01967 402257
Fax 01967 402041
email enquiries@kilcamblodge.com
Web www.kilcamblodge.com

Kilcamb Lodge is a beautiful and charming hotel which offers a memorable experience. The hosts are both hospitable and accomplished and the dining experience is superb. Local Argyll produce forms an integral part of the interesting menus which are beautifully prepared and presented.

SWINTON

The Wheatsheaf Restaurant with Rooms
Swinton
Berwickshire
TD11 3JJ
Tel 01890 860257
Fax 01890 860688
email reception@ wheatsheaf-swinton.co.uk
Web www.wheatsheaf-swinton.co.uk

The Wheatsheaf Hotel is primarily a restaurant but it also has a few very comfortable and well-appointed rooms. The restaurant has a well-deserved reputation for high quality dining in friendly and comfortable surroundings.

TAIN

Morangie House Hotel
Morangie Road
Tain
Ross-shire
IV19 1PY
Tel 01862 892281
Fax 01862 892872
email wynne@morangiehotel.com
Web www.morangiehotel.com

Morangie House is a very comfortable family-run hotel. Here you can enjoy traditional Highland hospitality, excellent accommodation and a dining experience which makes the very best use of the wonderful locally-sourced produce. AA Rosette.

TARBERT

Anchorage Seafood Restaurant
Harbour Street
Tarbert
Argyll PA29 6UD
Tel 01880 820881
email mail@anchoragetarbert.co.uk
Web www.anchoragetarbert.co.uk

The Anchorage Seafood Restaurant is a small, cosy restaurant which is rightly popular. The standard of cooking is superb and the local seafood, beef and lamb are prime items on the menu. A memorable dining experience can be expected here; the menu changes according to availability. Now under new ownership.

TARBERT

Balinakill Country House Hotel
Clachan
by Tarbert
Argyll PA29 6XL
Tel 01880 740206
Fax 01880 740298
email info@balinakill.com
Web www.balinakill.com

Balinakill Country House Hotel is a relaxing country hotel, smoothly run by attentive and welcoming hosts. The accommodation is very comfortable and the public areas impressive. Menus are well balanced and the ingredients are prepared and presented with great skill and care.

TARBERT

The Columba Hotel
East Pier Road
Tarbert
Loch Fyne
Argyll PA29 6UF
Tel 01880 820808
Fax 01880 820808
email columbahotel@fsbdial.co.uk
Web www.columbahotel.com

The Columba Hotel is a very comfortable small hotel which enjoys superb views over the harbour. The new owners have undertaken extensive refurbishment and the accommodation is comfortable and well-appointed. Cooking is excellent, whether served in the bar or dining room.

TARBERT

Kilberry Inn
by Tarbert
Loch Fyne
Argyll
PA29 6YD
Tel 01880 770223
Fax 01880 770223
email relax@kilberryinn.com
Web www.kilberryinn.com

The Kilberry Inn is a superb inn which has, quite rightly, been recognised for the consistently high standards it offers. This is a warm, cosy and welcoming place to enjoy delicious bar meals which use excellent local produce. The daily changing blackboard options are well worth considering.

TARBERT

Stonefield Castle Hotel
Loch Fyne
Argyll
PA29 6YJ
Tel 01880 820836
Fax 01880 820929
email enquiries@stonefieldcastle.co.uk
Web www.innscotland.com

Stonefield Castle occupies a stunning location with delightful grounds leading down to the sea. This is a traditional hotel which offers a high standard of comfort and ambience. The cooking is classical, uses quality local produce and is served in a dining room which makes the most of the location.

TARBERT

Tarbert Hotel
Harbour Street, Tarbert
Loch Fyne
Argyll PA29 6UB
Tel 01880 820264
Fax 01880 820847
email iain.robertson@tarberthotel.com
Web www.tarberthotel.com

The Tarbert Hotel is a traditional small hotel with comfortable accommodation. This is a friendly and unassuming hotel which offers traditional Scottish home cooking in welcoming and attractive surroundings.

TARBERT

Waterfalls Restaurant
The West Loch Hotel
By Tarbert, Loch Fyne
Argyll PA29 6YF
Tel 01880 820283
Fax 01880 820930
email westlochhotel@btinternet.com
Web www.westlochhotel.freeserve.co.uk

The Waterfalls Restaurant at the West Loch Hotel is well worth planning a stop at. Although this former coaching inn has a few comfortable rooms, the food and warm atmosphere are what attracts most people. Good use of local produce which is well prepared and presented.

TAYNUILT

Roineabhal Country House Bed & Breakfast
Kilchrenan, by Taynuilt
Argyll A35 1HD
Tel 01866 833207
Fax 01866 833477
email maria@roineabhal.com
Web www.roineabhal.com

Roineabhal is run by Maria and Roger Soep. The house is built in the style of a Swiss chalet and is cheery and welcoming. Guests are served with a set meal – only the best local produce is used and the cooking and presentation is both exemplary and enjoyable.

TAYNUILT

Taychreggan Hotel Ltd
Kilchrenan
Taynuilt
Argyll PA35 1HQ
Tel 01866 833 211/366
Fax 01866 833 244
email taychreggan@btinternet.com
Web www.taychregganhotel.co.uk

Taychreggan is a lovely hotel which sits in a splendid position overlooking the loch. The accommodation is well furnished and appointed and both the bar and dining room serve good local produce which is deftly cooked and presented with a contemporary twist.

THREAVE

The Terrace Restaurant
Threave Garden
Threave
by Castle Douglas
Kirkcudbrightshire
DG7 1RX
Tel 01556 502575
Fax 01556 502683
email khenderson@nts.org.uk
Web www.nts.org.uk

Threave Garden is another National Trust Property which is a delight to visit. The tearoom is a small and comfortable self-service operation where you can expect a tempting range of home baking, light snacks and meals.

TIGHNABRUAICH

The Royal at Tighnabruaich
Kyles of Bute
Argyll
PA21 2BE
Tel 01700 811239
Fax 01700 811300
email info@royalhotel.org.uk
Web www.royalhotel.org.uk

The Royal Hotel is a fine, family-run hotel which occupies a delightful position. You can opt for informal or more formal dining here – whichever you choose you can be sure of a very high standard – both cooking and service. A superb small hotel. 4 Star STB. 2 AA Rosette, 2 Star AA. Investor in People.

TONGUE

Borgie Lodge Hotel
Skerray
Tongue
Sutherland
KW14 7TH
Tel 01641 521332
Fax 01641 521332
email info@borgielodgehotel.co.uk
Web www.borgielodgehotel.co.uk

Borgie Lodge is a very popular hunting style lodge. It has been run by Peter

and Jacqui MacGregor for many years and they are experienced and accomplished hosts. The cooking here is of a high standard and menus feature local game and seafood.

TONGUE

Tongue Hotel
Tongue
Sutherland
IV27 4XD
Tel 01847 611206
Fax 01847 611345
email info@tonguehotel.co.uk
Web www.scottish-selection.co.uk

The Tongue Hotel is a superb small hotel which offers an enjoyable experience in every respect. The accommodation is very relaxing, the hosts are welcoming and the cooking is excellent.

TROON

Anchorage Hotel
149 Templehill
Troon
KA10 6BQ
Tel 01292 317448
Fax 01292 318508
email anchor1812@aol.com
Web www.anchoragehotel.com

The Anchorage Hotel is a very old, family-run hotel which has a particularly comfortable and relaxing bar. The food here is of a high quality and menus offer a range of traditional and contemporary dishes which are well executed.

TROON

Blueberrys Coffee Shop
3 South Beach
Troon KA10 6EF
Tel 01292 316171
Fax 01292 317294
email mmoug@shopscotland.net

Blueberry's Coffee Shop is a charming, friendly establishment. This is a popular meeting place and offers a good range of home bakes, light snacks and meals.

TROON

Piersland House Hotel
15 Craigend Road
Troon KA10 6HD
Tel 01292 314747
Fax 01292 315613
email reservations@piersland.co.uk
Web www.piersland.co.uk

Piersland House is a popular and elegant hotel which is set in attractive grounds. The accommodation is of a very high standard and the cooking is excellent, highly skilled and beautifully executed.

TURNBERRY

Malin Court
Cotter's
Turnberry
Ayrshire
KA26 9PB
Tel 01655 331457
Fax 01655 331072
email info@malincourt.co.uk
Web www.malincourt.co.uk

Malin Court is a bit of an enigma – it is a very superior private care home for the elderly but also has an excellent restaurant which is open to non-residents. The cooking here features excellent local produce which is skilfully and imaginatively prepared and presented.

TURNBERRY

The Turnberry Restaurant
The Westin Turnberry Resort, Scotland
Turnberry
Ayrshire
KA26 9LT
Tel 01655 331000
Fax 01655 331706
email turnberry@westin.com
Web www.westin.com/turnberry

Turnberry is a very special place and has charm and good taste in abundance. With new award-winning Executive Chef, Ralph Porciani, at the helm the dining experience in the Turnberry Restaurant is a winning combination of classic skill, French influence and excellent produce.

TURRIFF

Fyvie Castle
Turriff
AB5 8JS
Tel 01651 891266
Fax 01651 891107
email rlovie@nts.org.uk
Web www.nts.org.uk

Fyvie Castle is another National Trust Property which should be on your list of places to visit. The tearoom here has a great range of snacks and meals to suit all tastes – look out for the special Fyvie whisky cake!

ULLAPOOL

The Ceilidh Place
18 West Argyle Street
Ullapool
IV26 2TY
Tel 01854 612103
Fax 01854 612886

The Ceilidh Place is a wonderful and unique place. You can stay in the hotel or the bunkhouse depending upon your taste. The lounge has an honesty bar where you can make yourself at home after a long day – whatever you do don't miss dinner in the restaurant where you will be treated to superb Scottish food – fresh, tasty and skilfully prepared.

ULLAPOOL

Tanglewood House
Ullapool
Ross-shire
IV26 2TB
Tel 01854 612059
Fax 01854 612059
email tanglewoodhouse@ecosse.net
Web www.tanglewoodhouse.co.uk

Tanglewood House is expertly run by Anne Holloway – a highly accomplished hostess and chef. This is a unique guest house which is both luxurious and welcoming. Here you can enjoy the best of hospitality and superb meals – all using local produce.

UPHALL

Houstoun House Hotel
Uphall
West Lothian
EH52 6JS

It's easy to see why Houstoun House is such a popular hotel with its excellent facilities and high standard of accommodation. The restaurant serves very fine food which is presented in a classic style and uses good locally-sourced ingredients.

UPLAWMOOR

Uplawmoor Hotel & Restaurant
Neilston Road
Uplawmoor
Glasgow
G78 4AF
Tel 01505 850565
Fax 01505 850689
email info@uplawmoor.co.uk
Web www.uplawmoor.co.uk

Uplawmoor Hotel is an impressive small hotel which is expertly run by Stuart and Emma Peacock. Accommodation is very comfortable and menus in the restaurant are interesting and offer a good range of dishes which are all skilfully prepared and presented. Good Beer Guide. 2 AA Rosette. Silver Green Tourism Award.

WESTER KITTOCHSIDE

The Sheilings Café
Museum of Scottish Country Life
Wester Kittochside
East Kilbride
G97 9HR
Tel 01312 474383

This is a real quality visitor attraction which has a very good self-service restaurant within it. There is something for everyone here – from excellent home baking to a good range of snacks and light dishes.

WICK

Ackergill Tower
Caithness
Wick
KW1 4RG
Tel 01955 603556
Fax 01955 602140
email ruth@ackergilltower.co.uk
Web www.ackergill-tower.co.uk

Ackergill Tower is a luxurious and exclusive venue. The quality here is superb, excellent service and superb food – this is definitely a place for a very special or corporate occasion.

WORMIT

The Sandford Country House Hotel
Newton Hill
Wormit
Fife
DD6 8RG
Tel 01382 541802
Fax 01382 542136
email sandford.hotel@btinternet.com
Web www.sandfordhotelfife.com

Sandford Country House is a delightful small hotel ideally located between Dundee and St Andrews. The accommodation is very comfortable and the service attentive and friendly. The menus here feature much local produce and all dishes are freshly prepared and skilfully presented.

The National Trust
for Scotland

If you're looking
for great food,
in stunning locations,
try this for starters —
www.nts.org.uk

Be Different, Be Better

This philosophy has been the cornerstone of Baxters success and you can discover why when you visit us. The Baxter family, which is now in its fourth generation, have been producing some of the UK's finest soups, preserves condiments, pour-over sauces, fruit specialities and a wide range of other fine quality food products since 1868.

Today, the Baxters Food Group is one of the UK's premium food manufacturers, with over 150 fine food products and some of the country's leading brands to our name.

Experience the magic of Baxters for yourself when you visit us...

Baxters Highland Village welcomes over 220,000 visitors a year. Set on the banks of the River Spey, near the small village of Fochabers, you can experience the magic and success of the Baxters story through our audio-visual presentation and enjoy product demonstrations and tastings. You can also shop in style, choosing from a range of fine foods, cookware, clothing, gifts and other merchandise.

Baxters Ocean Terminal in Edinburgh is our inspiring store situated in the heart of the largest waterfront development in Europe. Stylishly laid out over two floors, there is a choice of shopping to suit every taste. Visitors can also relax with quality cuisine and enjoy the impressive harbour views in our Café-Deli or in our Fourth View Restaurant.

Baxters at Tullibardine is the home of our new flagship experience. In addition to outstanding restaurant facilities, Baxters at Tullibardine (below is a computer simulation of how it will look when it opens in mid 2005) offers a fantastic Scottish showcase of inspirational fine food, clothing, gifts and much, much more.

Visitors are invited to taste a variety of products, be it fine scotch whiskies, wines and bottled beers at The Dramming Bar, specialist chocolate in The Chocolate Parlour or tasting what Baxters is most famous for, speciality soups, in The Baxters Hub.

In addition there is a deli counter, coffee and ice cream bar and a cookshop, complete with a fully functioning kitchen for cookery demonstrations and tastings. Come and relax and enjoy our true Scottish hospitality.

Index

Index

Index

Index

Index

Index

Index

Feedback

Now that you have visited at least one – and hopefully many more – of the establishments included in Clark's Guide, we'd like to know what you thought of the experience.

You can register at www.besttastesinscotland.com and forward your comments that way.

Or you can fill in one of the forms on the next couple of pages and send it to:
Amanda Clark Associates
c/o Frame Creative
1–3 South East Circus Place
Edinburgh EH3 6TJ

Or you can fax it to 0131 315 0008

And if you have any other thoughts about the general standards of hospitality you received, tell us about them too.

Establishment visited _____

Date of visit _____   Meal taken _____

Comments _____

_____

_____

_____

_____

_____

_____

Name _____

Address _____

_____

Tel No _____

Fax No _____

Email _____

Feedback

Now that you have visited at least one – and hopefully many more – of the establishments included in Clark's Guide, we'd like to know what you thought of the experience.

> You can register at www.besttastesinscotland.com and forward your comments that way.
>
> Or you can fill in one of the forms on the next couple of pages and send it to:
> Amanda Clark Associates
> c/o Frame Creative
> 1–3 South East Circus Place
> Edinburgh EH3 6TJ
>
> Or you can fax it to 0131 315 0008

And if you have any other thoughts about the general standards of hospitality you received, tell us about them too.

Establishment visited _____

Date of visit _____ Meal taken _____

Comments _____

_____

_____

_____

_____

_____

Name _____

Address _____

_____

Tel No _____

Fax No _____

Email _____